Layers

New & Selected Poems

Introduction by Karl Orend

OTHER WORKS BY HARRY BURRUS

FICTION
Time Passes Like Rain

FEATURE FILM
Marrakech

PLAYS
Aztec Daughter
Prom King & the Fiancée
Machete
The Letter
Door
Siesta on the Río Rico
The Vanishing Oasis

POETRY
Cartouche
Jaguar Porfolio
For Deposit Only
Without Feathers
A Game of Rules
Bouquet
I Do Not Sleep With Strangers:
Confessions of a Tennis Pro

VISUAL POETRY
O!!Zone (Volumes 1-21)

COLLAGE COLLECTIONS
Oaxaca Stelae
Tanganyika Petals
Pátzcuaro Glyphs
The Jungle Is Feminine

Harry Burrus

LAYERS

NEW & SELECTED POEMS

ALYSCAMPS PRESS
Paris • London
2013

Alyscamps Press contact: Alyscampspressparis@gmail.com

"Marrakech Medina" by Bob Fariss.
"The Gabels in Thurburbo Magus, Tunisia" by Harry Burrus.
Houston Open Finals, Parade of the Crazies, and rear jacket photo by Megan Gabel.
"First Professional Haircut" by Wilma Burrus.
The front cover (*Inner Reflection*), collages (*Introspection; Oaxaca Stelae 51*) and all other images by the author.

Thanks to Mac Macoy of Phoenix for photographic retouching.

Special thanks to Samantha Rea for her ongoing help to Alyscamps Press.

Thanks to Arnaud Godineau for his continuous support.

Burrus, Harry,
Layers: New & Selected Poems

ISBN-13: 978-0615630458

FIRST EDITION

ALYSCAMPS PRESS
Paris • London

Megan

Marrakech Medina

In loving memory
of
Morris & Eleanor Gabel

The Gabels in Thurburbo Majus, Tunisia
Morris, Megan, Eleanor, and Randy

Introduction

Paris, in mid-December of 1994, was rainy and chilled. At Shakespeare and Company, overlooking Nôtre Dame, a few straggling tourists lifted the tarps covering old wine crates full of used twenty-five franc paperbacks, as a light drizzle fell. There were always good books scattered among the dross—an illustrated copy of *Last Tango in Paris* or *Quiet Days in Clichy*, a signed book by Ray Bradbury, slipped in surreptitiously by George Whitman to give an unsuspecting customer the thrill of a lifetime. In the early evening, lights from the chandeliers reflected from the sleek cobblestones as people scurried to make their way home, or to a lonely hotel room, a movie, or perhaps a date with a new woman. A few days earlier a sign was placed in the huge plate glass window at the front of the store—the window that George Whitman insisted we clean with warm water and old newsprint. Letters cut from yellow and white paper proclaimed "Allen Ginsberg Here Dec 13." Above them, a large black and white photo showed Ginsberg, unmistakable in his beard and glasses. A string of Christmas lights framed the whole and, beneath, stood a small vase of dusty plastic flowers.

On the appointed evening, Allen Ginsberg read from his latest book, *Cosmopolitan Greetings*, before a huge crowd. With him were his old friends from 1950s Greenwich Village, Shakespeare and Company habitués, jazz poet Ted Joans, and theater director and poet Robert Cordier, translator of *Howl*.

I did not linger that night as the crowd dispersed. A young woman awaited me, with blue-black hair the color of a raven's wing, and flesh, lightly scented with vanilla, pale as a ghost. She tasted of joy and oysters, and finally sorrows beyond end. Perhaps five or six days before, an anonymous man wearing jeans and a windbreaker and a tan Levi's baseball cap had passed by the store. A beautiful woman accompanied him and snapped a photo, in the background of which you can see George Whitman reading the Herald Tribune. Shakespeare and Company had been, for decades even before this photograph, first as the Mistral, then renamed for Sylvia Beach's bookshop, the center of the Anglophone literary scene in Paris. A steady flow of poets, novelists, literary historians and travel writers passed through the doors daily. Each Monday evening there was a poetry reading in the Sylvia Beach Memorial Library. The quality was uneven, but many gifted and famous poets graced these soirées. It was among these stacks that Lawrence Ferlinghetti and Gregory Corso had composed fine poems, that Langston Hughes and Ted Joans gave one of the most famous readings in the history of Anglophone Paris, where Jean Fanchette edited *Two Cities*, Merlin founders launched Samuel Beckett and *The Paris Review* found its feet.

The man in the photograph was unknown to all that passed him at the bookstore. He never sought out George Whitman to introduce himself or announce that he was a poet, editor, and publisher, known from Russia to South Africa, from New York to Australia, from Belgrade and Mexico to Peru. Perhaps it was modesty, or tact—a refusal to join the herd. George Whitman would have found much to talk about with this stranger. They were both world travelers and shared a belief in the redemptive power of literature, breaking down barriers between cultures, fostering talent and creativity and finding the extraordinary in the everyday world. Both had faith in humanity and a rigorous compassion. The quotation that graced the stairs at the back of the bookstore, "Be not inhospitable to strangers lest they be angels in disguise" was apt in his case. To many writers this man was a kind of guardian angel and sustaining inspiration. His name is Harry Burrus.

Harry Burrus is a fourth generation Texan. He grew up in Texas, New York (while his father studied at Columbia), and St. Louis. A gifted athlete like his father, Harry began to compete in tennis from an early age, eventually playing national and international tournaments. From the time he attended elementary school, he was interested in quests and journeys—which laid the foundation of his travels throughout the world as an adult. He began writing by developing a passion for recording his observations and experiences; the people, places, and things he encountered during his travels for tennis tournaments while still a teen. His observations were intensely detail-oriented, down to journal entries on the vintages of wine, style of china and brand of silverware in the homes where he was a guest. These entries led to poems and characters, and then to plays, and much later to writing screenplays, such as *Marrakech*. Books he read while still in elementary school in Webster Groves (St. Louis) were another important influence. These gave him an affinity with writers who traveled widely, lived life large, and pushed the boundaries of the socially acceptable. They included Joseph Altsheler, Jack London, Stephen Crane, and Mark Twain. He began to write prose as early as third grade, inspired by his reading and his regular Saturday cinema matinees. His interest in cinema from his teens was primarily European, including films by Bergman, Goddard, Fellini, Truffaut, Antonioni, Resnais, Losey, Visconti, Costa-Gavras, and Buñuel. Burrus developed a deep-rooted social and environmental conscience which is often reflected in his poems, screenplays, plays and fiction; and a fascination with strong and intelligent women, which led to him promoting the work of many female poets through his magazine *O!!Zone* and the decision to center his novel *Time Passes Like Rain* (2011) around the author Laura Ryder, with the backdrop of an (imaginary) adventure story set among the rainforests. Burrus uses the novel form to explore psychological, cultural, social, political, gender and environmental issues in a highly complex way that is reminiscent of other recent leading exponents of the novel and short story genres, such as Ismaïl Kadare and Paul Bowles. Two eagerly awaited novels are currently in preparation, entitled *The Hummingbird Wizard* and *Cambio*. Burrus has stated that he suspects "it is impossible to have any grasp of universality without travel, without placing yourself in unfamiliar terrain, and dealing with the challenges the unknown tends to place in front of you." This reveals movement, transformation, and flow as constant leitmotifs throughout his creative explorations of various mediums. Although it is perhaps in film that he finds the possibility of the most complete art form and structure, we should not underestimate his contribution to theater and the modern novel.

Harry Burrus has carried on an extensive creative correspondence, for decades, with various artists, filmmakers, photographers, and writers throughout North and South America and Europe. The specialty of his correspondent tends to determine the nature of the exchange. As a result, some know him primarily as a poet, others as an editor, filmmaker, collagist, playwright, or photographer. In 1993, Burrus founded the poetry magazine *O!!Zone*. It rapidly became one of the most important international literary magazines, with contributions included from France, Italy, Spain, Germany, Russia, Argentina, Mexico, Uruguay, Chile, and Brazil. It was through his new correspondents, such as Bob Grumman, Spencer Selby and Clemente Padin, that he became more aware of the international visual poetry and mail art networks, for which he was soon to become a major outlet and creative catalyst. Burrus began to contribute to mail art exhibitions and to incorporate stamps into his collages.

Harry Burrus developed *O!!Zone* out of a long-term interest in editing a literary art publication, which he had deferred for fear it would be cost-prohibitive. The magazine was initially a monthly, then a quarterly, and finally an annual publication—with an increasing visual and graphic element as time went on. *O!!Zone* was published in twenty-one volumes, copies of which are held at many University Special Collections, including the most important poetry repository in the Americas, at the University of Buffalo Poetry Center, in New York State. During its existence *O!!Zone* was the leading magazine for promoting the visual poetry of women. Its receptivity towards the most thought-provoking, candid, and provocative work, including the sensual and sexually charged, became a cornerstone of its reputation. These works were included, Burrus asserted, to "widen the emotional palette" and "enhance the integrity of the corpus." What he sought in his contributors were "distinct voices" that would "reveal something to me; to peel back the layers and expose themselves so that I may learn something about them or their environment, be it a tangible or imaginary landscape." *O!!Zone* rapidly established itself as one of the most widely respected creative outlets for international poetry.

Harry Burrus is the kind of creative artist, like D.H. Lawrence, who often has several projects underway at once, and feels equally at home in several fields of artistic expression. His need to express himself in writing and visually has always existed side by side, and is closely interconnected, hence perhaps his predilection for film as a genre. Film has, after all, drawn upon the talents of several major fiction writers, including Raymond Chandler, William Faulkner, and Norman Mailer. Burrus has always learned by reading and by watching others and followed closely Ezra Pound's dictum to make it both new and interesting.

Harry Burrus is the author of seven previously published collections of poems, numerous contributions to magazines and journals and four published collage collections. *Layers* is the first major retrospective of his entire poetic career and, as such, offers an invaluable insight into one of our finest American poets—a writer whose output has undeservedly gone underappreciated by the general public at home, while being widely praised abroad.

The poetry of Harry Burrus is highly diverse. It reveals the importance of visual imagery and movement in his imagination. In some of his poems, there are echoes of images experienced in the open street and of the close connection between everyday life, the written world, collages and art that were so important to Surrealist writers such as André Breton and Ted Joans. Shades of Breton's *Nadja*, Louis Aragon's *Le Paysan de Paris*, and Phillippe Soupault's *Les Dernières Nuit de Paris* are visible in his Paris poems. His poems of love are often poems of inquiry—a search for compassion and understanding of the other in a confused world. The quest at the heart of Harry Burrus' poetry is not merely a traversing of space and cultures, but also of time and of depth. He seeks to capture love in its various manifestations and to understand its mutability. Whether it is the love that is overwhelming in its simplicity and naturalness, as expressed in the poem "Song," or the shards of uncertainty and disintegration in "A Game of Rules," we feel that Harry Burrus has a profound understanding of the diversity and complexity of human connection—and our inner fragility. In fragments of momentary experience, he manages to capture truths that are universal about people and relationships. He insists on the difficulty, though never the impossibility, of truly coming face to face with another person. He is intensely aware that this only becomes possible in a naked awareness of our true selves and by making ourselves vulnerable to defeat. The same penetrating gaze is focused on places and diverse cultures. Many of his poems are informed by an awareness of other traditions. In one of his most beautiful poems "I Do Not Sleep With Strangers" we witness the transformation of an American into a cosmological being through his exposure to Buddhist thought and the purity of transcendental experience.

Harry Burrus is a consummate poet of love. His love poems are sensual and erotic, obsessed with beauty and that tenderness that exists when we are most able to see our ideal selves reflected in the glance of another. As a backdrop, images of water, of rain and rivers, often flow like passing time, like the honey from her sex, the tears from her eyes, the outpouring of our grief at that moment which can never be regained, merely vaguely remembered, and in which we at last found ourselves dead to the world and unified with all creation.

If you read the poems of Harry Burrus attentively you will realize that this is a poet of extraordinary vision, a modern day renaissance man, who draws upon a full palette of poetic styles to depict a picture of modern man and woman in all their complexity. He is aware that universal truths can be found in the most banal of experiences, if we can but perceive them. Harry Burrus knows that in each experience we also have the ability to recreate and reorient ourselves and the world around us. This is a poetry of vulnerability but also of hope, suffused with powerful imagery and a vivid imagination that never loses sight of the divine spirit within Man.

Fifteen years later, rue de la Bûcherie, another rainy night in Paris. I was once well-known here but am now invisible. I am even more anonymous than Harry Burrus that December night when his photograph was taken. This place is no longer the bookstore I remember. Familiar faces in the neighborhood are impossible to find. Memories flood in. Ghosts inhabit these streets. I remember back to how it all began. In my reveries, I realize that it was Harry Burrus, of all the poets I knew here, that had the best understanding of human nature and our place in the world. I adjourn to the place St. Michel, to a café from where I can observe young lovers and friends meet beneath the biblical fountain. In the swarming crowds, among the car horns and the sound of water running in the gutter I return to the poems of Harry Burrus. In this single volume, by one of America's finest poets, you will find an immensely rewarding vision of the possibilities within yourself and the world.

Karl Orend
Taos, New Mexico.

Contents

There and then, in the silence of the night, began the marvelous dialogue of the Chimera and the Sphinx, spoken in deep, guttural voices, now raucous, now piercingly clear, like voices from another world.

—J.K. Huysmans

Houston Open Finals

Tennis is transportation, taking us out of ourselves . . . .

LAYERS

Blue Mirror

He thought the white glove
of her memory would suffocate
by its own flame,
burning itself out like a suicide,
and she would forget
the amber memories their time imbued.
It was the best. For a time.
Better than anything.
Before or since.
If he could but loosen
the stones, overturn them,
so she could read the words
he never intended to write,
maybe then
the closeness would not be lost,
but could be summoned
like the anticipated smell of honeysuckle.

A Game of Rules

We Said Good-Bye

Someone breaks the silence,
but it is only pain,
like nuggets from a nightmare.

I translate myself into a burning guitar,
fluent in gypsy Spanish.
The dark moments come to me,
fibrous skin pregnant with wine, and I rejoice.

My black boots sizzle.

Under the sign of the goat,
we hold each other close
and make all lies evaporate.
From a large shell I hear the noise
of the sea
we have already sailed.
The shore opens its temptation catalog,
spreads it pages wide for me to review.
But there's no going back.

A thief clears his throat
and says
this is an Andalusian dance.
I don't know where I'm going.
But I will protect you from the others.
You must guard me against myself.

All this flesh is only a beginning.

Cartouche

Lyrics Chiseled by a Florentine

I guide my gondola
under Rialto bridge,
singing unrequited love songs.
Shutters are thrown open,
merchants abandon their shops,
leaving customers who want prosciutto.
Fish, learned in such matters,
swim on each side of me,
casting cold stares.
But my voice grows stronger;
my lyrics give hope to those hospitalized
and mesmerize chestnut vendors
who burn their hands and fruit.

The bells of the Campanile
ring out, greeting me.
I pass the Gritti Palace
while a mariachi band plays
"O Solo Mio."
It was like this in Cairo,
where on a clear, starless night,
I sang to the Sphinx
and answered all of its questions,
permitting it to lick my hand.
Camels from all over Egypt
left their masters
and came to the pyramids
to hear my song,
seeking a cure for their thirst.

I Do Not Sleep With Strangers

Where Have You Gone Café Conversation?

You are not here
where you should be, where we were
yesterday, discussing Sartre
and the rivers of the Amazon.

You left me hanging from a vine,
suspended above warm, murky waters,
piranha flashing smiles in my direction.

I'm sitting in the same corner
near the window, moping, watching
the worker ants pass by, full of Henry Miller,
Marquis de Sade thoughts, all directed towards you.

The lunch crowd has gone,
yet, you fill the room;
all tables say "Reserved," having only
your West Indies menu in mind.

I hear you crunching words,
I see your bright teeth chewing
my à la carte syllables,
your laughter satisfying surrounding appetites.

You were to tell me more
about my family tree. You pleased me
by pointing out my long life line when
you held my sweaty palm.

But why didn't I know my father
who saw me everyday? And why did
my mother only drink when she ironed
clothes in the basement?

There was a peculiar wetness to your technique.

You pasted my questions on my tongue before
the 8x10s were fully developed;
you enlarged everything, never losing clarity.

From outside, the pedestrians look at me,
as if I were a sundial telling them it's
past time to pop another memory pill.

I guess I'll sit here, pretending
I'm at the Deux Magots, reading my yellowed,
dog-eared Confucius, until the five o'clock
shadow informs me it's time to leave.

I Do Not Sleep With Strangers

Seed Lamp

Born to die,
we are the seed
of timelessness—

though
not of our doing.

Our reflection
from those deep
silver surfaces
shows us,
with cup in hand,
the darkness
we eventually
swallow.

There is no point
to measure
the time remaining
before our light
is extinguished, grows
dim, and fades to black.

The point is to savor
the peach's skin,
to ride
its flame.

Other lights will glow.

Without Feathers

I Am Told

I am told
your smile conveys more
than forgiveness.
Its ample weight sandbags
the rising bilge
whose center is a congested freeway
that has forgotten
what is meant by
an open road.

All routes lead
to and away from the heart.
Wings feather water,
saddled with the hope of being
home for a kiss,
a hot meal,
a warm bed shared
with another body.

I am told much
can be gleaned from a smile.
The bearer can be anonymous,
an abandoned shell
with a fixed expression.

It is the gesture

with its well-marked signs
that supplies courage,
that instills the will to continue
the climb,
to sign again
in spite of a fear of heights,
a fear of failure . . .
of saving face, of stepping
forward.

I am told
in a compact city,
behind boarded windows,
a room glows,
a red orange light trickles
from a throbbing, tracking eye—

a back door through night.

Without Feathers

Object Defined

I await the clear darkness
of your room. Outside
the chrome's blue, metallic eye
withstands our polarized reflection.
Without glare or haze,
the door swings open,
offering a skyline
by night,
a chandeliered close-up, silent
footsteps, wine
without blessing,
the river behind the formless mask,
three seeds
under the tongue
that won't grow.

I cannot see or feel the growth,
though I know some things
have changed.

A scrim shapes the moment
with its plain background.
The rain confuses
the tracks while
a white cloud passes
across the sun
and the first blade pushes
through without breaking skin.
I know more
than gestures are out there,
flying heavily,
buoyed by my questions,
a canvas without color.
I close my eyes and my branches.

Without Feathers

Museum Piece

From the moment I first saw you
in Florence, I've wanted one like you,

one I could call my own. For years I kept
the idea of you while I developed my skills.

When I determined I was ready, you served
as my model, and, while the wheel spun,

I drew the revolving clay up with my thumbs
and fingers, drawing up your sides to the desired

shape. Nature has not been my teacher.
I began by having less, at least not as much

as I saw in others, but I knew I would possess
and embrace you. Words would come later.

The firing took several days, three more
for the fires to die down, the kiln to cool

before the opening. Many firings were required
for the hardening, for the glaze and abstraction

of fused colors, before you could walk with or past
your maker, shaping all things to come.

Bouquet

We Are Gripped and Fascinated

Anger grows
without
a gardening tool.

The emotional prongs
are strong
enough
to become weeds.

Sitting here,
I imagine the white
refrain of your
blue blouse,
open,
your naked flesh
smiling,
inviting me in
without
a fee.

The fox crawls
away
from the tower
under a mist
of plain truth.

Between the
powder-dry flower
bed, sculpted
with inflexible aversion,
the wind speaks
in hushed tones
and makes room
for both of us.

Let's look

for signs
we can study,
like watching darkness
bundle
into sapphire
rubbings,
where the impression
left
is a large

moth with bones,
without a mouth
or heart.

Cartouche

Song

Every two hours or so, to break the monotony,
I pull into one of those scenic turn offs.
I walk around, stretch, and pour a coffee from my thermos.
I like looking into the distance, following the horizon,
to see how far I've come and to measure where I am going.
No matter which direction I face, I see you walking
out of mesquite, from behind green hills, or emerging
from a long expanse of bluebonnets. A half hour ago,
your face rested on the horizon line like a sun setting
or the moon slowing rising. This love of you is before me,
always, and in all directions.

Bouquet

Art Criticism

Puzzled by the clucking,
I looked out my window
and saw a Voice masquerading
as a green and blue parrot,
talking to a bearded man
who was feeding seeds to six
anxious pigeons.

The words floated
slowly around the vendor
like feathers, zig-zagging
towards the ground.
He would grasp a word,
here and there,
as if translating,
but complete thoughts escaped him.
Obviously, the language was foreign
and, not being a linguist,
he was able to complete
but a partial rendering
of a headdress,
like those worn by the Plains
Indians
of the American West.
In spite of the fractional
achievement, he seemed pleased
with his work
and stood on his tiptoes,
chin aloft.

The images
that passed through
the artist's fingers
turned into pamphlets
as they touched
the soft ground.

"Words, smoothly woven,
delivered by a masked orator
merit dissection,
contemplation,
and should not be
devoured whole,
no matter how ravenous
the hunter. Always look
for and read
the signs.
The water may be clear
and cool
and fatal."

I encountered those words,
written in Greek,
near Aswan, Egypt,
on a column of the Temple
of Philae.
Early,
but useful, graffiti.

Why, I wonder
the disguise of a bird?
Did the Word interpret
the act of feeding
as an appreciation
for aerial perspective,
a derivative of flight—
a keyhole
to the comings
and goings,
light
answering the dawn?

The parrot served
as a bridge for commerce,
an opportunity
for exchange, but

bartering was alien
to the man
with fixed prices,
despite his craving
for books
and tendencies
towards boudoir fantasies,
a trait not revealed by his song.

The Chief spoke
of sitting around a fire,
smoking the pipe
with white men.
And how an earlier vision
had shown a fire
devouring itself,
leaving nothing
that was known
recognizable.
The words they exchanged
that cavernous night
disclosed
what one could expect
from men
when they sit together,
telling stories
about their children,
about their children's
children. About
being brothers.

Did the preacher
stand on his toes
because he was proud
of his sermon?
Or
was he stretching
himself, reaching
for a clearer view

to comfort his preparation?
I think both.
And neither.
This behavior
is indigenous
to the cloth,
occurring readily
as heat
shares the flame.

I can no longer see
the man
or the parrot.
Both
have moved on,
becoming
something else.
The wind speaks
in concert
with a silver rain
that bleeds
the ink of feathers.
Only
a few pages remain.

A Game of Rules

A Girl Is A Girl Is A Boy

This year both of my girls are varsity
cheerleaders. I wonder if they keep
a diary? Is there any concretizing,
any tangible evidence of their thoughts?
Do my friends ever think about moral
obligations or maintain personal principles?
Should they?
This kind of posturing is part of you
without any preplanning
or contemplation of alternatives.
Who really asks what is out there
and wonders how they fit in?
I don't see the questions posed.
Our minds don't conjure
such intricate questions.
There isn't need.
It's not something we do.
What we do is react, react
to whatever stimuli we encounter.
Nothing more.
Day to day encounters determine
our truths.
We act out all the philosophies of men
whose names we've never heard of.
Few revelations unfold. We sit
on a slow burning fire and don't realize
what is being erased. What we see
and feel are not realities,
but sometimes we notice the pain.

Parkway High School
St. Louis
11 November 1960

For Deposit Only

Manchester Drive-In

Someone announces over the loudspeaker
for Sweet Pea to come to the refreshment stand.
Slowly, twilight expires
and the eyeless night spreads its dark curtain
over Manchester, Missouri and students
from the area high schools seek their positions.

I'm in the front seat with Pris,
Steve's in the back with Andy.
Cars are still coming in. Several roll
past our row, checking to see
who's with whom and such.

Steve and Andy whisper,
but mostly they're silent.
I look out and up at the immense blue
black river, forgetting for a moment
I am a high school junior, crazy
about a senior cheerleader,
honor student.

Sounds break the somber night air
like a dog barking somewhere.
How many guys I wonder are at the movies
with their girlfriend this Saturday night?
Thousands, perhaps millions.
How many are double dating?
Probably not as many.

Images begin to flicker across
the screen, parallel to my thoughts.
I look at this senior under my right wing;
she's safe and comfortable.
I hear *Save the Last Dance for Me*
coming from the radio of the red Ford Galaxie
to my left.

Entering from the neck, I move my hand
under Pris's sweater and slide under her bra.
My hand cups her right breast.
The back seat is quiet.
I imagine I am Michelangelo,
sculpting marble from Carrara—
a magnificent nude figure will stand
at the entrance of Parkway High School.

At home, full of tears, Pris runs
into her bedroom, jumps on the bed
and lies face down, crying.

1033 Kuhlman Lane
St. Louis
Spring 1961

For Deposit Only

White Skin Is an Idiom of Night

Snow falls on the road of my imagination.
Further south, barricades and thieves insure isolation.

Always I must confront the demons—
leeches sucking the spirit of its steam.

Each blast of smoke signals an alarm.
Without sleep or dreams, I will rid the landscape
of these carcasses.

I am flesh without flies or blossoms.
Breathe me.

The Candle Burns Without a Flame

Urban wolves seek flesh
and break glass.

The pulse of drums beats
across the polluted water
and inside the lips of diamonds.

Men and women drink
their future without a guide.

Only the fearless and free
cannot be bought,
but no one wants them.

Diérèse

Fairfield, Iowa

Strange the course a river chooses
    to make.
I had not anticipated being here,
not now anyway,
and under these circumstances.

15,000 is a small town.
Far removed from the East coast
and Eastern traditions.
Life moves in a straight line in Fairfield.

A trip to the post office
or Hallmark is a big event.
A few minutes and I've walked the town.
The High Lane Club and Cheshire Academy
are behind me. Two places
I'll never see again.

I have a few months of waiting
to see if Iowa accepts me.

Eggs sell for forty-cents a dozen.

501 Hillside Drive
Fairfield, Iowa
Fall 1969

Jaguar Porfolio

Tenango, Mexico

The village wells are dry.
Only smooth stones
occupy the river bed.
Quatla, a town thirty miles away,
dammed the river,
giving themselves more water.

Seeking aid,
Tenango's thirsty spend time
    in church,
praying for redemption.

A Texas priest
performs the mass,
forty-five minutes pass.

The parched throats raise
their bowed heads
and haltingly embrace
the bright light,
leaving their words as offering.

Unfortunately,
no water is served
in God's house.

Jaguar Porfolio

Thirst

I do not come this evening
to conquer your body.

I ask of your bed a dreamless sleep;
but first, that I might drink long

one of your mauve kisses.
Will we ever be a single body

beneath the ancient desert sky?
Perhaps, it favors me not to ask.

Jaguar Porfolio

We Look and We See . . . Sometimes

I need a drink from darkness;
I am everyone's parent.

Do you know me?

At dusk, they talk about the next morning,
dragging their happiness along with memory
while the river rises and fills the fields.

Every twilight, we choose to share secrets
through the clear lens of language.
I have walked far without you.
The calm chill fractures each body of heat
and haze like a glass or a dream.
Our palette with its myriad colors and smears
matches nothing.

                                        Small flames
float across your hooded grief.
No one sings.
I hear whispers scrunching over small stones,
each drama a flirtation, a pursuit, a preserver
for the uninitiated.

This is so beautiful, someone said.
But none of it seems to mean anything—
She went to bed with them anyway.

The swimmers lift their faces and gaze into turbidness,
searching the fathomless depths, and realize everything
there is to see
              is within reach,
but where does one start . . . and when?

Cartouche

I Do Not Sleep With Strangers

Ralph Litzinger was the second best
ball player on Cub Pack 306.
He batted clean up and had a crush
on my sister, Lei Lane.
Dad coached; I pitched; Lei Lane watched.
I always preceded my fast ball
with a huge Double Bubble bubble.
Even supplied with this tip, no batter
could get a hit.
A home run with my Louisville Slugger
put 25 cents in my pocket, Ralph's father
paid fifty. I always wanted the bases
loaded; a grand slam was a bigger pay off.

I grew tired of America's pastime,
thinking there must be more to life.
I donned my pith helmet and put on my favorite
British khaki, the bush outfit from Banana Republic,
and waded into the Ganges to be energized,
looking forward to spinning my first cotton shirt.
Later, I bathed in the brown, holy waters,
after first giving it a good boiling.

Possessing a knack for adaptation,
I quickly learned to interpret lotus blossoms
and to disguise myself as a tea leaf.
I observed that silence does not tiptoe by
like time. Silence is noticed and time,
like the shadow, dances to its own beat,
a pulse Occidentals are unable to find.

At the river's edge I met Gotama, the boatman,
and shared his pipe. We sat together, listening
to the river, overhearing running conversations
a thousand years old. Gotama shared his meals:
yellow perch, rice, and wild strawberries.

He taught me the habits of the river and how to think
in midstream. When we drank tea
he recognized my detached form.
He instructed me in meditation, tennis my mantra.

I stayed with him for three years,
ferrying people across the moving conversations,
hearing stories I'd tell other people's grandchildren.

When the time came for me to leave,
I was quizzed on the 1028 hymns of the Rigveda
and, by the potency of my words, he knew
I was ready. When we parted,
he handed me a red balloon, and asked for something—
a piece of Double Bubble and a quick demonstration
in the art of removing pink from the cheek.

To the east of the River Gandak
and north of the Ganges, an old Abyssinian
merchant befriended me.
Since I was adept at bookkeeping and fast
with an abacas, I helped him with his store.
At night he told stories about the Queen
of Sheba and how his great-great-grandfather
had played chess with Rimbaud.
He knew all of the beautiful women in the village
and the bicycle thief downstream.
He offered them to me. I said,
"I do not sleep with strangers."
The old merchant doubted, but accepted
my wisdom, and out of deep affection
presented his three daughters:
Jiva, Pali, and Gaya, who danced
and sang before me, trying every means
of seduction. All temptations proved ineffectual
and the Abyssinian knew
I was familiar with the Dharma Sūtra.

The years passed,

the seasons marked by the rains.
I saw where fortune and misfortune were accepted
equally, without complaint.

I continued to study and develop my skills,
I became quicker than the cobra
after tricking it and counting its scales.
And many times from October to May
when the trees lost their leaves
and the grass became parched and brittle
and wild animals died from lack of rain
I delivered water to the stricken areas
by changing myself into snow at night. At sunrise,
crazed elephants knelt at my feet.

The other seasons, too, had passed,
providing many turns at bat. I learned
that the bases were loaded and knew my moment had come.
I got up from under the Bodhi Tree, confident in my ability
to become a fine thing and to see the white white light.

I Do Not Sleep With Strangers

River

Shivering in the raw autumn air,
she walks to the water,
her right hand cradles her lower back.

Last night after making love several times,
her husband, still in bed and smoking a cigarette,
told her how good she was.
He said he loved someone else
and would be leaving.
She looked at *National Geographic*, thinking . . .

how he used to carve their initials in park benches
and leave notes for her on the sidewalk.
She always felt settled with him, believed in him,
and never had cause to doubt him;
for seventeen years love held her; he had
a convincing smile.

She awoke in the car, confused by the front seat.

This morning she removes her clothes and enters
the water, carried like a melon downstream,
easily she floats, she does not resist

as the river takes her far away
from the do-what-pleases-you city,
she is tossed over and around protruding rocks,
all becomes blurred; off to the right
she sees a sandy bank.

She grips the river's skin
and pulls herself to the edge,
changing her mind.

I Do Not Sleep With Strangers

Courvoisier

I've lived with the desire to grow old
with one woman, somehow knowing I'd lose
the one I wanted most. She had the beauty
of a French movie star, a Catherine Deneuve
or a Anouk Aimée. The bed is as we left it,
an abandoned campfire, cold as an indifferent sea,
disheveled with waves of books and bottles,
but most of all—her smell,
which is like the sun going down. I can't bear
to imagine her being touched by someone else.
Her lips giving another man a chance to discover . . . .
The candle on the table extends its reach,
writhing over the wall, in sync with the storm.
She loved moving in the rain, her skin glistening,
in and out of imagined spaces. Always the rain . . .
forming an endless backdrop to my saturated senses.
We had great zing, gulping down the happiness.
I loved when she tossed salad, brown hair loose,
hanging past her shoulders—wearing only that smile.

Bouquet

Koutoubia from Her Window

I spent each evening with her
that winter in Marrakech, remaining
in the medina until the early morning
light painted the city red. Her room
bled with saffron, lemon, and coriander.
She kept the shutters open, letting in
the Grand Atlas mountains, the minaret,
and the wailing echo of the muezzins.
She wore a hooded cloak, kopal necklace,
and veil. After a dinner of couscous or tagin,
we'd rinse our hands and drink mint tea.
In order to understand her better and for her
to trust me, I held her at a distance, knowing
all night moves were in the hands of Allah.

Bouquet

No Vacancy

Not checking in
at the motel desk,
Night enters
to eavesdrop
on all the rooms.

A hole
in his pocket
called Moon
guides weary motorists
to their doors.

Inside,
with sheets pulled
up and eyelids down,
travelers listen
to their subconscious,
unaware

their line is being tapped.

131 Selden
Galesburg, IL
1 April 1972

For Deposit Only

Who Can Say?

From inside
you see the shadow
of night
climbing out
of its cave
and you see lakes
collapse
into a desert mirror.

Rivers are held hostage
and the water strains
to seek another
level.

You see country
clubs in layers
of financial guilt
and clay courts
whose faces turn
away with embarrassment,
demonstrating a passionate lack
of social restraint.

You see women washing
clothes
inside of ancient fountains,
their limbs
the color of lost stories.

Men sit in dimly lit bars
raising glasses
to cracked, unkissed lips,

and with each swallow
their cataract eyes
turn more opaque

and then vanish . . .
leaving black,
empty sockets and

the sound of night dressing.

Cartouche

Jade Ghetto

Your tongue is the eye
I draw with—
enunciation of anonymous syllables.

I canoe through the wall's
underground chamber,
serpentine sleep of white blossoms.
Ashes line the shore—
and I listen
                    to your hymn
                              of lost virtue.

The mirror dissolves without a name
of its own.
The family tree continues
to grow and remains

invisible.

No one deciphers the bark
paintings falling from clouds,
escaping entrapment—

fragile crystals
exfoliating like panic,
relax all reins
in the name of desire.

I turn the pages of a pageless book,
tracing images of unwritten signs,
recording the voices
                              before they speak.
The names solidify and flash
back to a cherry kiss,
emptying the vase.

The prayer ignored,
all shells release an umbilical breath—

a chorus

in a minor chord,
in sync
with a lipless night
framed by a shard of glass.

Cartouche

Hocus Pocus

All the things she said, I wanted to hear.
I moved closer.
The rain obscured my view,
but the emotion struck high chords,
vibrating the lustrous gem,
and the room accumulated steam as vines grew
and dug into the living wall.

In the plaza, the sun lusts.
Aztec heat radiates beyond the eucalyptus
and the Gila monster leaves
silent markings few can read.

My words lacked the weight she wished to carry
for comfort and reassurance . . . a validation
for this year and the next, and the next. . . .

The mahogany statue splinters inside my palm,
a broken seed, flowering only if the wind does
its conjugal duty.

Inside the clock,
the sand drains hard without water to carry it
to the holy room, where lilies wait, limp
from inactivity, desire forgotten, misplaced . . .
somewhere in memory,

while the stained glass pulsates with multi-colored
interpretations of fountains without water,
and the final blessing is delivered—
a rote response to journey's end.

Cartouche

Crossing Styx

Excitement extends from my torso
like tentacles of a bramble bush.

I look at you,
at us,
our muted reflection
in the mirror,
wondering
how wide and deep
is this river
of chance.
I am thirsty . . .

your tongue slacks my ache.
I climb and hang
onto its leaves.

Others assure me
I have lost
all reason
because
of the way I guide
this small vessel
through
the interval storms.

The sky sings
its song clearly.
The clouds are a back-up
chorus. Its teeth
and nails are clean.

The whispers behind
the columns
do not dissuade me
from my mission.

The motive is for us
to join them
on an empty desert
coupling.

Let the sun
blister their shrunken
souls and fry
their anemic thoughts.
I will be
no one's alter lamb,
unless I choose to play dead.

And you know me
better than that.

Jaguar Porfolio

Spreading Wings

When truly alone
and swallowing the darkness,

the voice I hear responding
to my questions is uniquely engraved

as an echo of our conversations.
With the sand dollar you gave me,

I'm writing lyrics to a song
we'll soon sing. Knowing this,

I'll never remove the imprint
of your lips. Trusting you,

without feeling the imprisonment
of memory, I sign our name in water

for anyone to read.

Jaguar Porfolio

I Swim Upward

I swim upward
into the dark
cavern
through a narrow
side crevice;
the light
no longer bright
and clear
as it was
a few feet ago.
I must strain
to see.
I stretch my eyes
and probe

the dark,
slippery skin,
looking
for a clue—
a formation
to direct me
back
to that
volatile
eruption
of our beginning.

Nina Place
St. Louis
20 March 1967

For Deposit Only

Sleep

Silently, like a Sunday prayer,
the white falls, unseen, unheard—
like a leaf at 3:00 a.m.—
out and beyond the beveled glass
and French curtains, beyond the burning
wood as it cures the pale flesh.

Her long body stretched out,
her thoughts drift in muted color
as he occupies the thick bedding
next to her, dark and protective
like the night around them,
but unlike the behavior unraveling
in her blue, throbbing dream;
the oyster is empty, the pearl

already chosen, consumed.

Nina Place
St. Louis
3 April 1967

For Deposit Only

Knock On Any Door

I hear Popsie's footsteps
down the hall
and recognize his shuffle.
Hard to believe he's been dead since '62.
They were all there when I arrived:
Ronald, Uncle Ed, Aunt Ellen, Joab, Katie, Mom, Dad . . .
sitting in metal chairs,
forming a rectangle around the closed, dark coffin.
A rippling canopy shielded eyes
from the Lubbock sun.

*

I failed the math test Mrs. Botticher
gave in May of '57.
I climbed out of her classroom
window and went to Ken's
for French fries and a cherry Coke.

Ken was an ex-con
who could open all of our
combination locks.
He'd hold the lock in his left hand
and, raising it to his head,
would turn the numbers with his right,
listening to the tumblers magically
being whispered into his cauliflower ear.

That was seventh grade,
about the time I first considered
putting my arm around a girl.

I think a lot about Candy Cook's house—
the big painted brick at the top of Kuhlman Lane.
Inside they kept a monkey
that played with himself while eating bananas.

His name was Uncle. Outside, I picked irises
for the girls in my class.
They were always surprised when they opened their desks
after lunch. They never knew who put them there.

*

I shot my first hole-in-one
in Lubbock, Christmas '56—
six years before my grandfather's death.
"Don't Be Cruel" was playing.
That was five months before old Bottlewasher's
test. Little did I know I'd be playing
Charlie Gracie's "It's Fabulous" and
"You Butterfly" at Ken's, and I'd be changing
schools and never open that combination lock again.

*

Popsie, always the first one up,
loved his breakfast of Lucky Strikes,
thick black coffee, stacks of toast
dripping with butter. He enjoyed listening
to the news, the radio barely whispering,
so all of us could sleep. Sometimes, when I'd wake
up and join him, he'd talk about sports, baseball mainly,
that was his game. Grinning, he'd demonstrate how to keep
my arms in close when running the bases. I have his frayed
newspaper clippings; he was a star until a refrigerator fell
on his leg and ended his career.
He never did complain or talk about what he could have done.

At Parkway High, my State Championship
is still a record for the school—
won decades ago. Popsie never saw me play.

*

Last summer I climbed Kilimanjaro

and photographed the animals of the Serengeti.

*

Mornings, the neighborhood men were the first shoppers
in Burrus Grocery. They purchased a neatly wrapped brownie
that looked delicious. My favorite spot was to perch
cross-legged on the wooden check-out counter.

With the added height, I could see the aisles and the items
people chose; mainly, I felt important
next to my grandfather ringing up the sales;
he called me his "assistant cashier."

Those brownies were behind the counter on a shelf
next to the candy and cigarettes, beyond my reach.
My birthday was approaching; I asked Popsie if I could have one, he
said I'd have to choose between a brownie or a chocolate
cake, but he recommended the chocolate cake.
I listened to Popsie.

Lately,
I've been thinking a lot about those I've known,
who disappeared,
Popsie, who never took his medicine seriously,
and Claude Bakewell, my best junior tennis win,
who drove his MG into a concrete wall
his first Thanksgiving home from Princeton.

So much for turning faded pages—
it's getting late
and I promised Megan I'd meet her at seven
at the Pompidou.
She likes a blue dress
she saw yesterday in a boutique at Les Halles.
She may buy me something too.

I can still hear Uncle Ed saying,
"Let Harry see his grandfather,

they did a marvelous job on him.
He looks so good . . . open it."

I didn't think he looked good.
I'd never seen Popsie so still,
in a new suit, and wearing make-up.
It wasn't like him.

That's the only way I see him now.

I Do Not Sleep With Strangers

Number 6

Seven small
one level flats
one after the other
a straight line
A man
wearing white shirt
wrinkled slacks
white socks
sits in a chair
in front of his domain
He sits
watching
the cars go by
A neighbor
number 7
comes to the door
without a shirt
wearing wrinkled slacks
no socks
to get the paper
Later
he returns
in an undershirt
and speaks
to the man watching
The man sitting
nods his head
continues watching
No-socks
looks around
nods his head
returns
to his flat
number 7
On the sidewalk
a stooped-shouldered

old man
wearing suit and tie
slowly
inches
past
number 6
The man sitting
watches
the old thing
take
for
ever
to
walk
the
block
one foot
never passing
the other
He starts
to cross the street
but the cars
the man in white shirt
wrinkled slacks
white socks
is watching
force him back
to the curb
Finally an opening
Stooped-shouldered
inches
across
Standing
on the other side
he wipes nose
with hand
hand with sleeve
spits
on ground

dirty neat old man
who only inches
The cars
have all gone by
He
the man with white socks
still sits
in front of his door
number 6
watching

I Do Not Sleep With Strangers

Working Girl

She stood on the corner of Avenue Q
and First Street wearing a yellow dress,
looking bewildered, drippings from a grilled cheese

clung like cats' paws to her hem.
She would rent her looks given the chance.
Yesterday, she had a few hits, but none today.

Everyone is wearing a paper bag. It's early yet.

I Do Not Sleep With Strangers

Feral Tape

After dinner,
they climb
between mirrors,
isolating themselves,
putting up
a shield
of questions
to confound and intrigue
those
who contemplate
mountains.

There is as much
emotion
in that burst of energy
as in making love
the first time.

She was never happy
with acutance
of large image areas.
Typically,
soft edges would result . . .
dissolving crystals . . .
the intoxication of a kiss.

We enjoy
the subsequent disposition
and physical deployment.

A Game of Rules

You may think every picture you see is a true history of the way things used to be or the way things are . . . ain't it a drag to know you just don't know you just don't know . . . .

Hoss: Act One *The Tooth of Crime*

—Sam Shepard

Standard Tableau

A heavy rain enshrouds the town,
giving it a look of Maltese lace.
With hungry eyes, they walk
the tenuous side, looking for a door
or steps marking the way.
Lost in grey moments, gestures tag
the mind, punctuating soft holes.
Inside the cathedral,
no disguise is worn or discarded
until the exchange is whole.
A reverence for the past speaks
through the stained-glass window,
the fractured light pronounces each hue.
Outside, others search
for the strength of trees.
None of this is outwardly measurable,
not now, anyway.
Someone asks, "Does it matter?
If anything, what will be resolved,
and when?"
They become like so many
who are no longer together,
having heart, their stars, out
of sync, continue beating.

Without Feathers

Inside Winter

The intrigue comes due to the revelation
that the partially hidden
figure is similar to my image
and the strength of this may be
because it casts a projection
of the interior, unknown back roads.

Unmapped questions become a substitute—
a silver mirror for an inquisitive eye.
At night, winter's cry gropes
deeper than summer's and fills
itself with atonal sounds. Night
in winter blooms monolithic and black.

Without Feathers

Ramapithecus

A little guy who meant no harm.
Nourished by streams, tributaries,
major rivers . . . the endless seasons.

Your remains, entombed in fine silt,
prevent decay, encouraging
the gradual replacement of bones'
own chemicals by hard rock minerals.

You had not, yet, drawn in caves.

Three circumstances allowed you to be with us.
First, at the lake shore,
lapping waves throw a coat of silt
over bones lying in shallows.

You, without garments.

Second, beds of streams tumbling down
to the lake's edge,
permitting undisturbed sleep.

Third, streams near the lake water,
force it to drop its silt,
you continue . . . silent amnesia.

A river sliced gorge reveals your vertical record,
massive jaws, a short-snout . . . tools
of milky-veined quartz.

Little did you know how long you'd last.

A Game of Rules

Metering the Light

Her words are cold and flat,
like the sinuous tongue of a glacier,
instead of the ribbon of palm trees I had expected.

The atmosphere was not one of welcome.
Researchers mounted knives and rode bareback
along the tarmac, enlisting others to share their pain.

Everything was meant to be used, not just displayed
or stored. But, I am drawn to the image of a more authentic
life, far from rhythms of academia and starched poseurs.

In my mind, I had already taken the pictures
I expected to find, but, when I arrived,
many of them were gone. With dusk, dark voices flew

across the swept sky towards tomorrow's questioning.
When I look back, I think the scene looks familiar,
like a sepia-toned print. My anticipation was as white-hatted

as anyone's. Those were strong colors
for a tiny room. Thousands of bantam voices shout . . .
I hear them long before I see them.

The design range is broad, complete with windows
and a southern exposure. But the pieces seem bland,
in their place are other, more compelling images—

green terraces spun from an ancient cocoon.

A Game of Rules

Dinner at the End of a Rope

While waiting for bus 45
late one evening,
I heard a loud whistle.

I looked in the direction of the sound,
but could see no one. This was strange
since it wasn't dark. I then heard
a flow of Italian and turned to see
what was happening.

A man had lowered a bucket from his sixth
story window to a man below.
The man on the ground had just come out
of a bar, carrying a bottle of red Chianti.
He put the wine in the bucket,
tugged on the rope and up it went.

I could tell right off this operation
had been performed many times.
With great ease and a gradual hand
over-hand pull, the man above
brought his dinner home.

Via Bitossi 21
Mt. Mario, Rome
2 July 1965

For Deposit Only

Révélez

Es-tu aussi fort
et diversifié que j'imagine?

Tu es les mots.

Je te veux impatiente
et libre avec ton corps.

Alors, es-tu?
Peux-tu être de cette façon?

Montrez-moi et bientôt.

Hôtel California
32 rue des Ecoles
Paris

Ristorante

I have been to the same restaurant 3 times,
each encounter a different hour of the day.
Regardless of the timing, an elderly gentleman is always there.
His hair has receded and it's quite grey, almost white. I'd say
he's in his late 60s. Each time, he has worn the same clothes,
an old, dirty, grey suit which now is practically green.

He never wears a belt, his pants are too tight.
In fact, he wears them below his waist, and since these are button
trousers, he doesn't bother with the top buttons.
As a result, his middle protrudes a great distance.
Looking at him more closely this evening, I see he is wearing
a green sweater.
He talks with the proprietor, other regular patrons and occasionally
has something to drink. Food and wine are not the reasons
for being here; it's conversation.

There's a bus stop directly to the right.
After the bus makes its run, which may take ten to fifteen minutes,
the driver and ticket taker come over and join the conversation.
Their break always last longer than the run.
Several times, riders climb into the bus and shout at the driver
to get moving; he waves his fat hand and says,
"What's the big rush?" He lights another cigarette and rejoins
the conversation of pertinent issues.

Via Bitossi 21
Rome
5 July 1965

For Deposit Only

Trastevere

She has grey hair with yellow streaks.
The other femmina has orange-red hair
with bald patches on the crown.
Both have large stomachs.
They are not with child.
When they walk, it pulls them;
they stumble after it.

The husband of the woman with sparse red
hair constantly wears a hat.
He ignores his wife
who, really, is more of a companion.
He lovingly smokes his cigar.

All the men wear slick slacks—
shiny products of daily wear.
These gentiluomini are like their slacks—
worn smooth by routine,
not a rough edge to catch a nail.

La Cisterna
13 Via della Cisterna
Rome
8 July 1965

For Deposit Only

White Napkin

I'm sitting on a green iron bench
under an Indian Laurel tree
in the Plaza Borda.
Three feet away a young woman
in a red blouse and black skirt
holds her baby on her lap.
The woman smiles at me.

I open the conversation by asking
the age of her niña.
The woman glows and responds,
ochos meses.

She wants to know where I am from
and if this is my first time in Taxco.
I answer her questions.
I tell her I like the town,
the climate, and the people.
I find the perpetual crusading taxis
annoying and dangerous
since the drivers show no regard
for pedestrians.
She, too, dislikes the white VWs.

I ask if this is her first child.
She nods. She poses questions
about Mexican states and is eager
to participate in the conversation.

The baby makes a small sound and presses
against her mother's camisa.
The woman unbuttons her blouse
and positions a dark nipple in the child's mouth.
The little one makes loud sucking sounds.
A tiny hand pushes the shirt open further.
She has an appetite, I say.

The woman beams.

Something moves to my left;
I see a large white butterfly—
a flying servilleta—
do a slow-motion flap
across a fuchsia bougainvillea.

The enfant finishes dining
and promptly closes her eyes.
The dark-eyed woman wants to hear
about Michoacán and Chiapas.
As I tell her about San Cristóbal de las Casas
she shifts her position and her open blouse widens.

Her caramel breast is the most beautiful piece
of architecture in the zócalo.

Friour Review

Finessing the Nuance

The miraculous comes so close
when the bed pulls back its hemp sheets
and petals catwalk the sticky dew.

The suspense fades in the corridors
of glass buildings, like clouds passing the moon.
Our bones fill the liquid space
as the sun bakes the higher ground.

The alley's neck strains to touch the nectar.
The field erupts with phantoms and it's not yet spring.
Your lips gather all my branches
and for once, agree with my suggestion.

The forgotten one waits in the burning thickness.
She is patient, but considers others.
She will sleep when the first apple falls.

In this veiled country, the gathering begins.
We must smother the doubt that separates us.

Bend over my taloned warrior.
The eyes of lightning suture all wounds.

We must dance past the fools.

Cartouche

The Sunflower Marries Air and Song

If we could suddenly float off into space,
if we could connect the first time
with spicy words and juice the white field
with plum-skin urges,
maybe then the land would breathe and sustain us.

I would feed you fluids from the nectar of ripe fruit,
pluck your feathers,
and teach you the luxury of pain.
Nothing shocks me,
certainly no words or phrases nor memories
swamped with bones of forgotten conflicts.
There is no need for translation or to monitor the echoes.

I have left a trail of fire.
Let your dreams resurface.
They are the heat that steams
the image,
shapes it,
and outlives
the form.

Call it ivory.
Call it pearl.
It is like you—

call it Perfection.

When you fall, all I touch twitches and becomes firm.
Soon, you will release birds and leaves without veins.

If you wish, cry out.
Nothing is forbidden.
Not with me.

Summon everyone from the perimeter

who has earned a velvet trail
and not been fattened with lies
and the recollection of midnight skin,
or the ambition to become someone else.
I will light the paper and dance the sacred parts.

Give me your hand.

We have not yet reached the nearness of our end.

Cartouche

Curtain Call

It is 6:43 pm.

I'm outside in the carport
waiting for Megan.

A few houses down someone is cooking
steaks on a grill.

A ribbon of pink serpentines
across the pale blue western sky.

The Houston darkness begins its descent

and slowly envelops me
as I watch the trimming

chase the narrowing patch of blue.

China Doll

After several months of waiting,
she became like a desert:
a study of contrasts
and contradictions, a shifting dune,
moving endlessly without direction.

She kept my letters in a jade box.
With her, I didn't see what I thought I saw
and my words reflected what I'd seen.
She traced our problems to a piece of blank paper
going into water, an image coming out,
complete with masks and unmarked distances.
How do you decide what to say
when you know seeing comes before words,
and the relationship between what you see
and what you know is never settled?
You can't start with an idea.
The explanation never quite fits the sight;
in or out of darkness, the hole remains.
Ours was an intense merger, an adaptation
of a fixed perceptual landscape,
the most fertile I've ever had.
Although I've said that before
and meant it each time.
After we had been there for a while,
she confessed she was angry.
She clutched her breast and said,
"I don't want it to be over."
This was the instant I had been expecting.
I suddenly realized I was witnessing it.
She showed me an elegant room,
richly appointed with oriental rugs,
wainscoting, a fireplace;
in the center was a drawing table
that held an open book.
A man had begun to walk from the page

onto the table. He looked at me
and I gazed into my own eyes.
A cloudy sky formed the ceiling.

Danger lurks in these kinds of journeys . . .
getting so involved with someone's life,
you forget what you're here for.

A Game of Rules

Drive-in

Whenever I defer to stasis
or envision a blank screen

to exercise meditation,
the image is always there:

a back yard full of transparencies
haphazardly arranged, so,

every way I turn demands a wide stretch
to black, into a quiet sea where chills

anchor my drifting. I've tried to forget
what was once a promising shoreline.

A Game of Rules

Agreement

I don't want
from you

what others
have had

or what you
have given them.

I offer you
my visions,

my humor, and
a willingness

to always go
for ice cream.

Bouquet

Offering

There were no direct moves on your part.
You didn't approach me the standard way,

by using corny lines or adopting a come hither look.
I knew right away there was much we could share.

What I'm saying may puzzle you, since, you don't
know me, but I'm convinced we are a treasure.

We are of the blue ground, a flawless diamond,
only to be cut and polished. It is up to you.

I've come to you because your fine brilliance
etched itself deeply, reaching my center,

captivating me. I was unable to turn away,
and didn't want to. Many couples speak, but say

little, their words caught in a powerful undertow.
They are powerless to save themselves. Your

image dances, moving in fifty-eight facets, a sun
casting no shadows. I see you clearly,

a magnetic force pulling and pushing me to you.
I like the way you move, cutting and giving shape

to space. I like the way you carry yourself,
shoulders back, confident, and strong. . . .

Together we will uncover ancient markings
and, with one of our edges, carve our name.

We have not discussed the obvious and I appreciate
that. Your eyes tell me we know many secrets.

What we have is rare.
Do not be frightened by this precious gem.

Bouquet

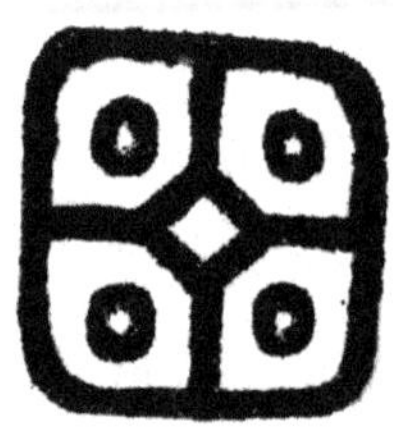

Souvenir

I meant to
send you a bud

from the Pin Oak
outside my window,

but
I knew

you wouldn't
want me

to sever the branch.

Bouquet

A Game of Rules

He stops walking, looks up, and becomes confused.
It's as if the other blue were the water
he expected to find, reflecting
all the good he'd been through. Instead,
he saw he was encircled by a colorless wall,
transparent from bottom to top.

He decided to see the wall as a player
in a chess game, not as a barrier
to break his disposition, but something
to keep his mind limber, challenged,
besides, he could direct the movement of his own thoughts.
Had he not proved before that he was unbreakable?
To hell with them.

As soon as he spoke
of places with four or five
syllable names, I could tell he had knowledge
of uncommon things . . . places I'd read about
or seen in the movies
starring Jeff Chandler or Peter Ustinov.
He amused himself by creating his environment.
Using chalk, he sketched figures on the wall:
a dying animal had collapsed, its legs no longer
able to support the weight of its body;
yet, its head was lowered as if in defense
against attackers. We moved in close
to see if the work had been completed.
For him, like Stone Age man,
image and reality were indistinguishable.
He wanted both within his grasp.

Some say she ran out on him; others say
he was too aggressive, neglecting her for the cause.
Anyway, it was before the trouble started.
Each day at sunrise before painting, he recited

the last conversation they'd had together,
he spoke both roles fluently.
At night, every night, he acted out their first meeting.
Gradually, the sentences became shorter,
the words only a whisper.
Soon, I thought, he'd have to improvise;
He speaks a different language already.

Lying expressionless on their metal-framed beds,
they continued to dream about dreaming dreams
with star-filled nights, fireworks, birthday parties . . . .
It was on a Wednesday, at sunrise,
he spoke his last words,
words uttered with a thick accent.
No one pretended to understand him, even then,
although something about him looked uneasily familiar.

Out of the blue, she, too, thought of him.
She'd read somewhere that each love
experience was, somehow, a part of every love
a person would have. But she didn't see how
that could be possible, since each experience
and each person were so different. But, why
was she thinking of him, now, and at twilight?
Could it have been triggered by the trip to the zoo?
The unusual conversation at dinner?
Or, could it be the mural he painted
so long ago still wounds her,
still haunts her, reminding her . . .
it all seems like hunting for big game.

A Game of Rules

Untainted

A sheet of glistening lances
shields the mysterious lady.
Without warning, lightening flashes
highlight her body,
creating a hot silhouette—
a chant of distant drums
negates the clear silence . . . and
glass tears melt skin in timely fashion.

She emerges, confidently
a personae from antiquities—
a fine wine to decant,
a subject of penetration,
someone to ask
about the erasing of shadows,
someone to . . . merge with fire,
someone to burn love with.

Iowa City, Iowa
12:30 a.m.
7 March 1970

For Deposit Only

Check Point

The line raises itself
coldly, methodically,
and without looking.

Rain hammers away
as if to mend the broken pieces.

The others are kept waiting
for hours.

It's all so ridiculous.
No one will admit it.

I remember when the line
first covered itself
and responded to the cold words,
which were not delivered with the intent
to hurt, but more to define a stance
and to establish a jumping off place.

None of what I say softens
the act
and, each moves forward
away from meaningful dialogue
into a haze of silver-framed promises
everyone owns.

It's so much easier to meet at the Panorama
and knock down a few Herraduras.

Semana Santa 1971
San Luis Potosí
Hotel Progreso

Jaguar Porfolio

Who I Am, Who I Was

Constantly, like a gloom-filled coffin,

memory shackles me to the past,
even though much of it has withered

and the rest I've buried, deeply,
as I wanted to long ago,

but lacked the courage.
Burnt whiffs of smoke still rise

from those ruins tainted with death.
Everything I did and said keeps

circulating—scattered ashes
reinstated by the wind,

reminding me what I was,
reminding me what not to become.

I continue to listen
and move closer to the fire.

Jaguar Porfolio

We Are Who We Are . . . Mostly

Her enthusiasm need have meant
nothing more
than
I needed a warm presence.

Something in you
attracted me
to her. . . .

For a second she forgot
where she was
and saw only the empty glass
waiting
to be filled.

Why this anger?
Her earlobes flexed.

Something you said
reminded me
of the specific circumstance:
an abrupt, unplanned departure.
All siren songs
stick in my throat.

I recall a splash of red.

A note sailed from the balcony
into waiting hands.
There didn't seem to be
any way
out.

We were caught.
Our flesh exposed.

She grew bored
having to explain
herself.

A fey haze clings to crimson
faces: someone guilty,
someone insane,
someone stupid,
someone innocent—

anyone,
someone poor.
Each a lovely presence
to be measured.

The wind blows
adding boundaries
so that
in saying something,
something else unfolds.

She stepped out
of the shower and
looked at me mockingly.

"I don't care," she said.
I've reached the end."

The door was unlocked
and we filed in
and I said
since we have tried everything else
we might experiment with truth
and whatever comes after that.

Cartouche

The Prophet's Speech

Two hearts
of palm
rest
on a
brown table.

A marble bust
wearing
sunglasses
looks into
the sun.

An aqueduct
casts its shadow
across the
cobblestone
streets.

A crow walks
out from inside
the colonnade's shade.

Its wings
do not break
the blue

packaged silence.

Cartouche

About Face

In a lifetime, a face faces a legion of faces
and rarely do we show our noble face,

the beautiful fresco we consider the principled
likeness. Which one should I show you?

Which one can I show? Situations such as this
always depend upon the circumstance. What

kind of moment are we having, need I ask?
How often do you show yours, your unlayered look?

Sometimes, one face reveals another, another
layer, previously undiscovered; sometimes the other

face reveals one's own. And, if this should happen,
we are making progress. By removing the veil,

you have exposed my unfeigned face and I will
relinquish it, only to you. This, indeed,

is another look, a sincere one, unlike the others.
There is a look for every look, a face for every

face, regardless which one you wear. And wearing
a different look helps one to understand one's own.

I'm wearing your face most of the time; I've
grown to love it. Besides, I like the look.

Bouquet

Speaking Chinese

Late evening
Early morning

Broad smiles
Talking eyes

Two half moons
A full moon—

My hands grasping

Bouquet

Absurd Hour

Midway in the cluttered room or facing
the crevice where the walls touch, I am alone.
The door confronting the outside light is open,

but only darkness snakes its way through.
I find myself isolated, the separation not from
any action I have launched. In this empty space,

the quiet amplifies the dark sounds and the only
beam of stimulation is remembering you. I thought
I was a brave man. But, I feel like a madman,

fearful of emptiness. Why am I alone? What have I
done to have to ask? What is it that tortures me?
I used to pretend I was higher on the pedestal

of some paradise . . . that we loved in a country
beyond dreaming. Will all of my longing, all of my love,
make a difference? I am a corpse placed in an open

coffin—a ship caught in the doldrums waiting
for a breeze to infuse motion back into its body.
Is this lifeless space my life without you, my life

with love drained from it, our light extinguished?
This can't be happening. Has this frightening, absurd
event occurred . . . or is my imagination playing

sorcerer, casting a warning, underscoring the meaning
of appreciation, demonstrating the penalty for self-indulgence?
Am I left only to see you in my dreams,

never to touch your face? When and how will I know?

Bouquet

Caminando

The sun is high
and sweat rolls down
my forehead and arms.
I pause to catch
my breath.

The cobblestone street is steep,
a 45 degree angle
and I'm at 9,000 feet.

To my right a woman grinds
corn soaked in lime water
on a stone metate into dough.
She shapes the masa into small balls
and pats them into tortillas.
She places the round cakes
on a comal to cook.

Behind her, under a tin roof,
a child wrapped in a woolen blanket
sleeps on a cinderblock bed.

Two sides of the casita have walls.
One is tin,
the other strips of wood
with open spaces.
Two gray kittens mew
at the señora's feet.

Friour Review

The Violin Has No Strings

The grass smiles at its reflection
in the low hanging clouds.

Footprints lead away from the bloody scene.
Today, death is a rainbow, the white light gone.

Travel does not imply escape.

The numbers are staggering.
We outnumber the animals in the zoo.

Blackbird

The Dawn Aches for More Sleep

The tree robs the spring
of its blood.

Within days the words
are forgotten.

Soon, a new fragrance
will be imagined
and a new portrait drawn.

Do not disappoint me.
Sing,
nothing is more important.

Blackbird

Within Reach

Fearing an endless fall
through silence,
each hand gripped

the white leaf as it floated

out of the cloud and into the morning
conversation which rested between
an exclamation of bitterness and hunger.

Diérèse

The Water of Air

No more cold demons confront me
in the steel mist of a misplaced hour.

I am shooting the curl, riding the barrel.
A moving, lined medusa replaces your bedroom
eyes and warm body.

Jellyfish guide my feet.

The mind breaks up without conviction
and shapes are full-bodied and everything
keeps adding up.

I can't take it lightly.
I don't want to—I cannot.

Wings extend and guide me through
the absorbent blue and silver language
towards the abyss and transparent aching.

Without regret I continue to sleep.
My eyes close like the bolt of a door.
My astral body floats—
a butterfly above the highway reflecting the sea.

My balloon throws away its braces.
There are no crutches in the Pacific.

Growing

The sun's clear, diaphanous like white wine,
she, a reflection, not belonging to any
particular object as do shadows. She left,
a leaf, suddenly taken with the wind, a coppery explorer
searching for a place to change colors, a place to dream,
a place with a different name.

I thought of her as my woman, possessing all I'd ever want
or need, my mantle of evergreen; instead, her dynamic lay
in expectation. I wonder if the warmth I feel
is that comfort of enduring companions, something
I instinctively feel, but don't have.
Maybe, it has to do with wanting to see people dance.

I Do Not Sleep With Strangers

Pink Curtains

The building is white

but because the light
is sliding down the other side
of the world, it looks
robin's-egg blue.

The shutters and door
are open to room nine.
The desert wind moves
pink curtains.

One set stretches
through the window
like a tongue
reaching for something sweet.

A single ceiling bulb,
like an afterthought,
warms
the rose-colored room.

I decide to enter
so when you walk by
I can invite you in.

I Do Not Sleep With Strangers

A Light, A Bridge

Saturday, 3:30 a.m., Misty Meadow, your room.
A portable fan shook its head—
you lay next to me, no longer a stranger,
someone who agreed hours earlier
          to be at risk.
My fingers played . . . arpeggio, one note after the other.

Time as solvent has divided us; you have returned
to a sepia tinted landscape, your surroundings
diminished in saturated color. "The person that left Wroxton
is not the same person that lived there. My spirit was not
          with my body."

You have rendered me buoyant, unable to sink.
I am glazed, jumping from tennis and family
          to the suddenness of you.
I could lose myself in this De Chirico canvas.
Your image seems to sit on the surface
of darkness; it doesn't seem to be part of it,
the way a gum print has an ambiguous presence
as though it's not sure
whether it wants to be a photograph or a painting.

You, too, squeeze out of absence, roughing in,
blending with violet to red waves; your unbuttoned blouse
comfortable with my smell, my touch, my words—
a montage covering your unabridged skin.

Sometimes, I'm compelled to recreate,
so, I sketch, slowly, deliberately,
forming a trompe-l'oeil, using deep, even breaths.

Your lips in my palm, I place my cupped hand
to my ear as if holding a conch shell
and listen to your Baccarat words come shattering out.

The bridge doesn't connect often,
its voice remains low, it hides anywhere, and
waits before selecting, before merging the lights . . . .

I Do Not Sleep With Strangers

Hôtel Maison Dorée

3 rue El-Koufa

The guidebook had said spotless,
rather formal with antique silver
and china used for breakfast and dinner.

Our room is small and dusty
and hadn't been cleaned in weeks.
No mattress, just a box spring
on three wooden slats, set far apart.

The pipe under the bathroom sink
and the taped pipe to the toilet leak
when turned on or flushed.

The Tunis twilight beckons.
We go out to walk rue de Hollande.
The crowd moves steadily, but mechanically
as if walking in slow motion—
a trek without hope—
a food line wanting bread.
The palette is minimal.
The men wear grey and muted brown suits.
The women, too, lack color
and wear dirty white headscarves.

Tomorrow, after breakfast, we're changing hotels.

Mirror Image

What is it that pulls
us to the past?
Certainly, curiosity plays
a major role—but what is it
that we are looking for?
Some morsel of dirt-covered
information that prompts an epiphany,
moving us in a new direction,
possessed with fresh enlightenment?
Unlikely. Maybe, whatever is gleaned
only goes to reinforce how unchanged
we are and that all the basics still apply.

Yes, I'll Go

This
is about going
with a white feather

that sailed
through my window
and landed

between your breasts,
resting
on the whitest part.
I've decided

to follow
its lead
and separate
your valley
with my own
plume
of intervention.
Keep
your window
open—

you will
know when
I arrive.

Jaguar Porfolio

By voyaging to the end of the imaginary, one can create a rigorous, experimental, and very real object, a document more truly in touch with actual events that a strict reportage of those events could ever be.

—Jean-Luc Godard

Loaf
(Visual Poetry)

```
                         LOAF
                          #1


          F    s    t    h    a    g    a
          o    o    h    a    c    e    s
          r    m    i    s    c    t    s
               e    s         e
                              p    o
               t    b    b    t    f
               i    e    e    a    f
               m    h    e    b
               e    a    e    l    y
                    v    n    e    o
                    i              u
                    o              r
                    r



Crack     open      the     egg
crack:              wisdom
destruction         aborbs
of                  you must extend frontiers
others                              of
continues                           self-doubt
                                         is
                                         no
                                         excuse
                                         or
                                         a
                                         reason

                                         not
                                         to
                                         act


Who makes the rules?
     Who rules the jungle?
          Who rules the street?
               Who rules the government?


B-E-C-O-M-E  A  F-O-R-C-E

                                    or
```

Offerta Speciale

LOAF
#2

```
d   f   g   i   s
o   e   e   t   t
n   a   t   s   a
t   r   t       r
        i   a   t
        n
        g

        c
        l
        o
        s
        e
```

Sever the yolk
remove all burdens
the egg
must be penetrated
she claimed
if you want us to experience

GROWTH

Mommy Daddy

INT. CONVENIENCE STORE - NIGHT

Denny Wong did what they asked.
Wong received a 9mm slug for his efforts.

Traffic remains clogged
on the north loop
where a 14 wheeler overturned.

Why did they have to shoot him?
asks Benny's father.
Why shoot him?
shoot him
shoot him
shoot

SCRAMBLE THE KILLER

Offerta Speciale

LOAF
#3

```
I   w   I
    h   t
d   a   s
o   t         t
n       m     o
t   h   i
    e   n     t
h       e     a
a   h         k
v   a         e
e   s
```

Wally Smith discovered his wife cheated on him.

He wasn't pleased.

Took Wally 2 years to make this detection.

Wally's favorite ice cream is chocolate swirl.

INT. WALLY'S BEDROOM - NIGHT

10:30 p.m. Wally sits on his bed eating a pint of ice cream.

At 10:20 he beat Gloria to death with his *Louisville Slugger*.

Wally wanted more,

but he has his limits.

One pint a night.

Offerta Speciale

LOAF
#4

Show me
yours
Ill show you
mine

reluctant at first
Estelle unbuttoned
her blouse.

She liked Mack.
He kissed real good.
Much better
than her husband
Larry.

Larry bowls.
When Larry bowls
Estelle sees Mack.

Mack's an addict.
Makes no difference to
Estelle.
Mack treats her right.

Tonight
Larry told Estelle he rolled

2 4 3

That's great Lar said Estelle.
Want some of this cottage cheese?

Offerta Speciale

LOAF
#5

```
s   s   l
o   i   e
    t   t
e
a   b   t   o
s   a   h   t
y   c   e   h
    k       e
t           r   g
o   &           u
                y

                d
                o

                i
                t
```

None of my friends would wear this.
I want to be like them.

I want to be liked.

I want to go out.

It's important to be popular.

It makes school tolerable.
Otherwise
it's all reading
and
numbers -
crap like that.

Somethin' else . . .
I could use some gas money.

Offerta Speciale

Conscript

Grey clouds move slowly across
the waning crescent like cattle

and step, once again, into dark
pastures. My breath leaves me

and hangs in the air like crystalline dew.
From my window I hear night calling,

summoning my subconscious spirit,
asking it to turn away, to walk out

from the awning of clear, lucid day.
It's asking me to shed my mindful

clothes and run madly, wildly,
and not look back at the security

on the balcony. I can hear the moon's
steady rhythm, the waves marching

to the shore, endless, endless soldiers.
How horrible to believe in nothing.

How lovely to welcome other voices
and to listen to their songs, while dressed

as a soldier, and you pressing against me.

Jaguar Porfolio

Laughter of a Perfumed Storm

In the night of the beginning,
I climb and crawl
    for the power
        of conjuration.

Fireworks ignite. A bouquet
of daisies wilts in a blind
    doll's hands.

She celebrated no birthdays
she can remember
and has no memory of color.

Where sleeps the shadow of children
in a cave of line drawings,
erased
except in the eyes of hunted animals?

Their cries infuse words
and the mark on the sundial
composes a forgotten song
as a pregnant dawn

flowers

an open door,
burnt by waiting,
amplifies my silver reflection.

Cartouche

Any Name Will Fit

So much can come
from a single moment
and it often blurs
with time.

Such is the way
the mind settles
things.

The effect shades
whole distinctions
and the wall's ear is out
of tune.

Each stone
inhales the
crisp light
and the wind carries
assumed names
as introductions are
exchanged
and fried like
bananas

in sizzling Mérida.

Cartouche

Cathy's Lament

Out her window,
she could see
her yard
full of dandelions.

Seeds and weeds
spread so easily,
like tiny parachutes,
she thought,
as he
continued grunting,
hands
gripping her shoulders,
his sweaty chest

4 inches
above her breasts,
8 inches of him
pumping her

while her blue-eyed
Siamese
squatted
in its litter box

and her mother's high-pitched voice
left still another message
on the answering machine
on top of the cedar chest
next to his burning
Kool cigarette.

Cartouche

Migration

I'm sitting in my patio at 1266 Fountain View Drive.
The wind lifts our banana tree's immense leaves
and for a moment, one I want to prolong,
I hear a rogue elephant's four foot ears flapping
somewhere deep in the Serengeti.

I look out beyond our campsite of three tents,
a cooking fire, and a bucket-on-a-rope for a shower
where Megan tries to refresh herself,
and I watch the migration of elephants, zebras,
and wildebeests, en route from Tanzania into Kenya.

As I watch the parade of these magnificent creatures,
I think of my father whom I have seen once since 1973,
the father who has progressed from age 52 to 72.

An envelope from his second wife with 10 cents postage
due arrived today. Inside was a recent Florida newspaper
clipping with his picture, no words from either of them.

There are no words from the animals, but I continue
sharing parts of their journey, only, I move about
singularly with my mate. . . .

My herd dispersed long ago.

Cartouche

Resurrection

The line stretches within its borders;
its bloated underside cries
out for sustenance.
Its hollow orbits ooze
blurred images
tabloid fashion—
souvenirs
of handmade origin,
no longer clearly formed
or recognizable.

Thousands of swollen lips pout
with rejection.
The orange blaze's whip cracks
the skin
and like the once proud
terra firma
lapses into crevices of acceptance,
extending hands, begging
for absolution.

The saturated palette lisps
pale,
like the bleached landscape
that hasn't been renamed
or claimed.
Scorpions covet the memory
of darkness.
The elephant sky trumpets
a summoning for lines to gather.

White powder positions itself
in
long,
even
rows,

stripped bare,
ready
for the hungry
takers
who crawl
down
from
the barren hills,
biting hard
on rolled bills—
a knife between yellowed teeth,

anxious to see the face of God.

Without Feathers

I'll Send for You

The white sand
on and on,
lit by a sliver of a moon.
The violet Pacific
pounding.
She, in her sweat-
soaked hammock,
naked
as the eroded cliff
below,
bites into a dream
she clings
to:
their first home,
built of plaited bamboo
and thatched
with woven leaves
of coconut palms.
She learned about
possessing
by being
possessed.
She cannot
remove him
from her body.
Their first
meeting
he handed her
shells
marked
with the names
of islands
he wanted
to photograph:
Easter, Pitcairn,
Fatu Hiva . . . .

When she walks
the beach
and looks
far past
the blue,
she imagines,
before falling
asleep,
that they lie
and inhale
the exhalation
of the surrounding forest—
mouth to mouth
with the breathing
greenery,
one
inhaling
what the other
expires.
Her life,
exploration
and discovery.

Just one
believes
the promise.

Bouquet

The Guide

It's gratifying talking to you,

listening to you speak of places
you've been, where you're going.
I wonder if I will ever leave.

I grieve about my past. I hope
my life will change. Never
leaving home closes me in,

not open as you are open. I strive
to alter my awareness by reading,
listening, observing you, growing

with you as you grow. Trouble stirs.
My stomach churns; I fear you
will leave, my exit to the other side

then closed. I'll remain locked,
confined by my surroundings, a cocoon
waiting for the precise moment.

Bouquet

Aplomb

The dark sky, the flash
above the street lights,
again and again,
like the Milky Way . . .
the virtues of loose brushwork,
rich color.

She was with me last night,
contriving erotic situations
built for arousal . . .
for the sake of sensation,
threatening
to wash me away
before achieving.

I did not expect otherwise,
but the urgency and complexity
of our feelings
bred a sense of uniqueness.
I collapsed before
I could take hold,
the scaffold long and narrow.
Perspective is not important
unless you estimate distance.
I wanted to transfer to the other side,
to see
eyes open, wide,
the first time,
to hear the morning breathe,
to feel the rain against her laughter.

A Game of Rules

Apprenticeship

He wishes the evening had unfolded differently,
dark and moist, with husky repetition of murmurs.
He should be more practical. I like to say
I have no use for such things.

A few believe inability produces amplified pain,
a chorus singing,
a guillotine complete with stains.

They break the fields in cold silence,
turn over the layered story, the parchment moves;
the lions distinguish themselves;
everyone gives . . .
after first taking what they can—
doves with the beaks of eagles.

Their belief lacks concern for detail.
The color of this portrait is something inexpressible.
The ideas fade; they attempt to catch it directly,
attempt to see it. But, in order to attempt,
they must already possess it as such or how could they know
what it is they want to see?
For some, it may end well,
catching the object through the order of its qualities.
But it's too early to really tell; many are absent.
The comparison passes behind the thing.
The mist begins its stretch; the curious respond.
Without a strong shovel, nothing will turn over.

I can see a backdrop of golden fires
silhouetting old men who sit replicating, whittling songs.

Thinking of Luxor
From a Midwestern Obelisk

Without being coaxed, she removes her babouches,
takes off her caftan, erasing any doubt;
my misgivings scatter like grain
winnowed by a farmer. Her Nefertiti eyes glow,

disclaiming any allegiance. Her perfume
compels me to question the remaining veil.
She performs the ceremony sitting cross-legged
in front of me, the dying light disappearing

into her dark mask. The mosaics cool our hot skin.
Grasping a wooden mallet, she crushes almonds
into a paste, her eyes, a study for the West.
Using a clay jar, she prepares sugar water,

the white crystals, ancient barges on another journey.
She stirs the liquid with a long, wooden spoon,
adds orange blossoms, mixes the almond paste
with the water, strains it, and pours into

the earthen bowl containing ice which she offers . . . .
Such rich moments of silence,
naked as the tombs on the other side of the river.
The ability to make almond milk is a gift,

outwardly there are no proportions, no rules
for the taunting nectar to emerge.
I let her vanish into the streets, fuse into the day;
having tasted, I remain curious, unsatisfied.

What has happened to my heart?

I Do Not Sleep With Strangers

Intending to Forget

The mist crept in over the north pond,
touching, wanting my attention.

Each droplet held a starburst of moonlight
like my wife's wedding veil, her eyes gleaming

beneath the Valenciennes silk, the stained-glass
windows, the warm, reddish glow of first light.

This is the cathedral with its mosaic of images, friends,
and amplified sounds, spiraling—nature's kaleidoscope.

I am a viewer of beautiful forms.
I lifted my head, surprised, again that I was alone.

I wonder, would she be thinking of me
in a place like this, dripping with silence,

wet with memory, remembering how strong love was.

I Do Not Sleep With Strangers

Anchor

I had the game deboned
before serving you.
You may proceed to chew. Swallow
without fear; nothing will harm you.
Your beliefs, like your words,
ran over the edge,
onto the valley floor where the people
whose hair is all lengths, all colors,
were caught napping,
unaware that you had finished
your silence. The crowd begs
for consolation—your shadow
vanished hours ago. They are ready,
whenever you call.

How well you weave
the dark poppies into an arch
of ambient light. Some call it faith,
the others . . . well, they follow,
without questioning. Each walks
through the festival of seasons,
past the leaded windows,
past the tangled vegetation,
past the sea wall, and up
the face of the mountain,
ignoring all landmarks,
but chanting the names.

The line pauses, the procession ceases;
you contemplate a meadow.
They talk of building the inner vault—
this displeases you.
It is not between shadow and space.

They cross the velvet bed
that muffles their footsteps.

Miles away, the sound is amplified
through a shell; your decision has spread.

Please,
there's no need to hide.
They wait for you to spend the night;
they fill the corridors with flowers
so the dust cannot gather.
They will banquet on baked leaves,
until the ashes no longer breathe.

Their instruments are quiet,
and while your memory remains in their mouths,
sleeping like a seed comfortable with winter,
I will take you where the air is clear,
where your voice will fly through rain,
where the light has no end. Come.
My heart is shoreless and can divide into halves.

I Do Not Sleep With Strangers

Soothsayer

The ruins are well-known
in this part of the country.
And it is equally understood
he contributed to his own
pleasurable destruction
in order to insure his charted
history would be studied
by bearded men who'd sit
in poorly lit buildings,
on high stools,
making pronouncements,
accompanied by sweeping gestures,
about the dark periods
of behavior and self-indulgence.
And how, on the extant columns
it is written:
"The cultivation of the rose
is necessary in a reign
to establish faith and order,
    without which
no study of art would ensue."

No one who knew him
would pass
his pale, painted face,
but the others were impressed
with the smile.
Such is history as he wanted it read.

A Game of Rules

Unconscious Suggestion

You come home when boredom is ripe.
You change from climbing office politics
and go into other things that are not
hand to hand.

You stare at the base of the lamp
and look out at the dying evening.
You light a cigarette and postpone
talking. You pour another drink
and wonder what you will do
when the next time comes.

Where will you go while everything
remains undone? The rooms of friends
are out of the question.
Black wires race past.
Reluctantly, you stop for gas.
Always for cheap wine and motel rooms.
You pile your refuse into the bed ocean.
You enjoy the sounds beneath you—
the bed shadowed with the smell of body
resin and storm clouds. You don't care
about public worlds.

I am enough of a stranger to put my hand
in your mind's pocket. How many suns
have set since you emptied them?
Later, you said you were dreaming
of guns and heard children's voices.
As you moved closer,
you saw their faces were old.

Without Feathers

Search

With eyes closed,

I see you
with my fingers.
You are canyon
deep,
multicolored
stone,
smoothed
beyond the scope
of hands.

Words, too,
sculpt an image,
each carving
I embrace.
Clouds
shoulder your lips;
the wind tears
the ice. Thawed

questions penetrate
the white
blue white,
and the crow
traces our journey
through
each season,
unwatchful
of the curving end.

Without Feathers

Order to Go

I grab the broom
and sweep
the discards
of last night's party
into a dust pan,
along with broken cups,
paper plates,
and partially eaten pizza.

I pick over
your left over words
that linger
in the disheveled segments
of my mind,
assorted pieces
of rejection
sprinkled with anchovy digs,
not the kind of treat
I want to reheat
or experience again.

It's true,
you've got my number,
and it's being called
now,
but after being served,
I don't want to go
to the end of your line,

and wait for another turn.

Jaguar Porfolio

Savanna

Unlike the grasses, I am uprooted.
My design—to grasp what's above,

beyond my vision, relinquish connections,
establish roots below, and parallel.

I appeared first in Denver, five pounds,
a small thing, easy to control.

I'm moving towards center, away from
the box designed by paternal hands.

I travel light, no encumbrances
of incubation. The heavy tutorial days

with their horrid nights; those bags
I no longer pack. I can't go back,

thanks to the white mountain.
Her light washes and bathes me, removes

my Father's residue, the taste of the
terra firma he gripped each day.

Her beacon guides me to inner rooms,
chambers I never knew existed, only knew

through unsettled nights, the wet, flashing
dreams. Unlike the grasses,

I am unraveled, dispersed
continuously . . . in all directions.

Jaguar Porfolio

The Hush of Indifference

Where shall I stand
now that the sand has absorbed the music?
You can bite me. I cannot let you die.

If only I knew with certainty
those of you in the crystal fire
who come here out of spite—

our art is tribal.

We are dragons, frozen when silence speaks.
Our deeds are words in midnight lace,
frost no longer a pretense.
Coming together, we praise the hearth and home,
a thigh warming embrace tingles
and adheres like ice to the tongue.

Sky to earth, I am here to celebrate
with an appetite for intimacy—
a warrior ready for battle.
This is the hour.

I am a leopard in a slender body
of memory, playing my conjure box,
cursing my lack of innocence—

anxious to dine.

Alto Alentejo

The train arrived at five.
The only way to get into town
is to take a taxi and I just missed it.
I drink a few beers at an outside bar
and wait for the taxi to return.

Later, I walk the 16th century
cobblestones, go in and out,
up and down the labyrinthine streets
and arcades and sit at the edge
of bubbling fountains.
I drift to Caesar,
thinking how he called this place,
"Liberalitas Julia."

I take pictures of the Temple of Diana
and project myself back to the first century
as my fingers trace
the Corinthian granite columns.
I admire Diana's fine physique
and wish her well.

I am obliged to bend to enter the door
of my 15th century convent
room, disappointedly bare
of worshippers. Quaint. But,
I was looking forward
to a demonstrative discourse
on conversion—heathen style.
Good view of the ramparts, however.

At dinner, I sit under
a Manueline fan-vaulted ceiling
near an ornate Moorish doorway
(which leads to the Chapter House).
I begin with sopa, an omelette de Jamo,

followed by fish, cerdo on skewers,
pollo with green beans & potatoes,
flan and torta for dessert—
feeling more Roman by the bite.

I have a café in the small bar
and raise a toast
to Hemingway with a Fundador.

An American couple gives me a look—
not of merriment.
I hear them complaining
about the small, old-fashioned rooms
with dated, wooden furniture,
the awkwardness of the doorway,
and how the place looks like a monastery
or something . . . not like a real hotel.

I turn my attention to a discussion
on television
about cinema vérité,
realizing it's rolling
through the camera, right now,
two tables over.

Pousada Dos Loios
Chambre 21
Évora, Portugal
4 September 1974

For Deposit Only

To Faro & Talk of Nuns

8:35 a.m.
and I'm on the bus to Faro.
It's a long ride,
but I'm sure the southern exposure
will provide insights to the natives
of Baixo Alentejo and the Algarve.
I'm counting on it.
I plan to engage in frank conversation,
discussing the
Five Love Letters of a Portuguese Nun,
that is
if
I can locate a nun
willing to talk in a confessional way
and avoid the church litany.

Beja. Here for two hours.
I take a cab to El Centro,
find a spot where I eat two sandwiches
and drink a beer,
all the time watching
the movement unraveling before me:
a man with a paralyzed right arm
dressed in an orange coat and tie,
hair brushed back,
face, a leather tan,
tries to sell flower seeds.
Five feet away and I smell the garlic
that encircles him.
Many old women are dressed in black—
witches crisscross the streets,
thousands of miles
from Kansas.
But no one's heard of Dorothy.

Back at the bus station,

I pass women cooking
on braziers on their front steps.
None that I ask has read
Lettres Portugaises.
A man passing on a donkey claims
it was written by Count de Guilleragues.
He asked,
"What do nuns know about such things?"

And that was the extent
of my first-hand exchange
regarding the epistolary classic.

Rua Capitao Joao F. de Sousa
Beja, Portugal
5 September 1974

For Deposit Only

Daily Catch

Slept till ten.
Looks like a cloudy day.
I call for breakfast, write postcards,
sleep a while longer.
I notice the tide is out—
comes back at 3:30.
Go for a walk to get mineral water
and stamps, inquire about transportation
to the beach, also ask about flights to Malaga.
The Friday afternoon fishermen
come into the harbor next to the hotel
and deposit their harvest. Earlier,
from the balcony, I could see them
digging while the tide was out.
They anchor their skiffs
next to each other and empty their catch
into burlap bags and straw baskets;
a few put the catch in nets.
Most bring in clams and other shellfish.
Several change pants, maintaining
excellent balance in the rocking boats.
Three put on slacks over long underwear.
Dressed as salesmen, they hop-scotch
from boat to boat to the landing.
They put the sea fruit in two-wheel
carts similar to rickshaws and push off
to the restaurants, ripe for escudos.

Hotel Eva
Faro, Portugal
6 September 1974

For Deposit Only

Dining with Des Esseintes

As I enter the 2nd floor Trafalgar
restaurant on Rua Monopolio,
I flash to Des Esseintes's trip
to London, aborted after his English
meal in Paris at the Bodega tavern.

A mustachioed Englishman,
in a blue and white stripped shirt,
greets me at the top of the stairs.
He wears a long, thick gold chain
with a Greek coin that hangs
to the middle of his chest,
his shirt unbuttoned to his belt—
obviously proud
of his robust physique.

He seats me in a black leather chair
in the bar,
one of the two rooms of the restaurant.
I drink a gin & tonic,
preview the menu,
and decide to wait for one of the two
balcony tables to clear.

All I hear is the King's English.
I look around, take in the pink
complexions, and plain-looking women.
Definitely English.
No one laughs or smiles.

My food comes: vegetable soup, garlic
bread, pork, and stuffed squid.
Below me, the street activity picks up,
mostly strollers looking at menus
in restaurant windows.
Many locals sit at outside tables,

drinking wine, smoking.
One, in a beret, looks at his buddy
and points to several female tourists.
A mother and daughter on the adjacent
balcony are saying they can't understand
why more of the Portuguese don't speak English.
The mother, in a blue suit with lace
collar, sends the wine back twice
before she is satisfied,
nods appreciatively,
as she swills the Château Latour,
the daughter busy with her oxtail soup
and smoked haddock.

I return to Des Esseintes.
Outside, it's pouring, inside,
the English stare into their liqueur glasses.
I have a coffee laced with gin and ask
for the bill.
Time to leave.
I tell the cab driver Hotel Eva.

At the rooftop bar, I drink a Fundador,
listen to guitar music, and review
my London visit, thinking of Hong Kong,
and a beauty in a Suzy Wong dress.

Hotel Eva, Avenida da Republica 1
Faro, Portugal
6 September 1974

For Deposit Only

The Bachelor Stripped Bare by His Shadow

And afterwards
he placed the white mask
on the table with bamboo legs.

He could see the carpet was dirty.

She hadn't found the mask
amusing,
nor worthy of the occasion—
even though
she was a woman of the theatre.
She thought he was acting
out of character,
that he was being specious.

The mask, pretending to sleep,
opened
one eye,
then the other.

It had to take a look
at this woman through its own windows,
not those of its patron.

It panned with her
as she crossed the living room
and entered her bedroom
while the young man sat
quietly probing his mind
for glimpses of happier moments:
the skyness of the sky,
the treeness of a tree,
the housiness of home.

It was the essence of things
he sought,

because when all that was peripheral
was omitted,
he was left free to imagine.

Cartouche

The Slice Disconnects the Skin

Lying in the silent furrow,
I don't think about language
forcing involvement.

Breath means pondering fragments,
small scarlet pieces,
even bold feathery ones—
scented messages of blood.

I propel lips
along the inner thigh of columns,
dripping the globe
like tear-filled handkerchiefs.

It's night, day, morning,
afternoon . . . somewhere in
Botswana or Brazil.

Inside tight fitting skulls,
a floating eye reminisces.
The wind's indifferent
and spins barriers around us—
many walls display messages.

The fire utters its final words
and writes its legacy.

I walk on through,
ignoring rumors,
releasing the fragrance.

The rain sings and takes it
slowly,
enjoying the strangeness
and the strange,
listening to the heavy breathing of gills . . . .

I take a bite of fleshy melon.

A knife is a dangerous gift.

Cartouche

She Sleeps in a Rainbow

To usher in your story
the boarding planks bend
double
and you prohibit machines
from clanking and cursing.

Men plunged by song
and
pierced by flame
sit naked by the fire,
toasting genitalia nostalgia.

Many withdraw,
wallowing within the orchid
wheel of an addict,
as if dying,
anticipating
the ugly months ahead.

Few maintain silence
against the overwhelming vapor.

Teens saunter off
together
and plunder everyone
with jism eyes.

Cries from the territory raise
a naked story
into chronic fever.

A négligée, half-open
like a blasphemy,
disappears and plots a course
inside a neighbor's eternal absence.

None protest the confetti.

A few drag the command
of a chrysanthemum

and bathe in the shadows
of forgotten copulation.

And in accordance to what
might have been,
threadless walls struck by sunlight
and air
spiral hungrily towards me,

my consolation chalice in hand.

Cartouche

Equilibrium

I sleep suspended on a web of silk.
A Zulu warrior crouches
in the tall grass. The tower flashes
its beacon across the landscape
and your spear glistens
in the cold dawn.

I try to reach the hourglass
to turn it
over,
enlisting another cleansing,
but
it is too late.
Moths flee from my open bureau
and
glide beneath the door,
seeking
the yellow glow of life.

My lips crack and bleed
as I try to speak,
their metallic shine signals
the waiting ship outside the bay.
A fisherman glances at his watch
as music plays
inside conch shells.
A cup of songs overturns,
extinguishing the pressing light.

I rub my eyes and the sand
scratches the mirror, leaving more
words for me to read.

Without Feathers

Phosphorous

The wall's blank face slides
across the room and drinks
in the shallow light of the tree
whose wide-spaced eyes swallow the fire,
the water, and roll backwards into
its sockets to read a memory blooming.

Without Feathers

Chance

My hands
remove the skin

covering your body,
clothe you

in tactile impressions,
and uncover the skin

of our skin.
My hands

greet
the wanderer

whose blood
I claim.

Without Feathers

Looks Like a Young Thief

I can tell you are ready.

The young birds no longer seek
and offer no explanations for their behavior.

Today they struggle. Tomorrow, who knows?

The racket and grind chagrin the conservatives
as they embrace predictability.
It all figures according to the accountant.

Collected sweetness makes nests
in basins by utilizing desire.
The sky with its vast throat comes
to the conclusion you must turn your back
completely, if only to prove to rivals
the leaves have finally turned.
So, let's get on with it. Grab a rake!

Ignoring custom, many reject dogma
by using bread and water, an easy technique
to get past a difficult situation.

Speaking of returning to your situation,
relax in a death-defying mode.
Confess or say nothing.

The graduates peer inside fortune cookies.
They've lost their grip and there's a ruckus behind me.
Try to imagine ugly banalities
and a scandal-plagued ceremony.

Stasis threatens.

Most of us cannot see the eventual
absorption encircling our most precious behavior—

pink meaty nipples rub against tall ladders.
Which rung will I get hung up on?
Get past?

Everything is so clear in the dark.
Why protest?
The angels bless everything we do

and a sweet and peaceful wind blows.

Treasure

Near your lair where summer sleeps
encircled with silver roses—

good friend—

I search across the river for your lips.

My questions climb: direct and far
from what is false;

and soon within another
file, another Spring, another knife,
the blade cuts through the white lace
displaying a delicate touch,
opening the dryness of your mask.

Soon come the Fall's mellow brown . . .
lost virtue,

and limp reflections. Each are thrown back
into the endless rooms of forest mirrors,

and suggestions,

where silk sheets hide the past
and oil portraits cry.
A torch lights the space and a stone with many names

scratches a tableau marking a new beginning.

Jaguar Porfolio

Strings of a Protracted Statue

The largest crowds
are drawn by the storytellers
whose green hue
of exterminated loveliness
reveals a yellow stain,
complete with petals
looking in
the looking glass for another look
for definitive names
that fall
flush
upon the precocious skin,
a steely blow—
but nothing can be as frail
as coquetry.

What dress?
What springs
analytic with a glimpse?

What hand endlessly rouges
for the dance of the evident
smoke that anchors both
great and small?

I pose these questions and
in vain
the seasons hold
their lovers
beyond the deposition.

Where you have gone
farewell apparitions are seen
with scorn.
The impulsive,
the goodly red, the fire,

the last kiss,
suddenly
there is this desperate path,
a way
to endure
like a confused attack
of wild seagulls.
Examining further,
deep within
the blood's horizon,
odds-on pick undresses
faint stars
with
expressive metallic sounds,
reverberating visions
of the sun and the sea
in one precise moment of clarity.

A jade eye emerges
from the unhinged
held in abomination.
Our seed discharges
into the mound
where skin and sobbing
fever prepare us
as a spoke in the kaleidoscopic wheel
of this moving away reality—
ash that must be
spread across the earth,
arranged according to features
and functions, irrespective of size.

Am I to go on kissing
a name on a wall,
looking
at a picture
from a determined characteristic
of a sleeping state?

All the forgotten provide
an indication of
where I would exist
in a distributed,
altered state.
I exist there
like a ferocious animal
with more
than one exclamation of surprise.
I am a witness
without the mirror reflecting the fire.

And when the sea
has completely entered
the disk of the winter flower,
its degraded acid will meld into a statue

of voluptuous memory, provocative to touch.

Jaguar Porfolio

The Garden

(Envisioning Megan)

I have concern for the figure
moving away from me as in a dream
into another room where I, too, want to go.
Not because I want to see the room.
I wish to be there, since she is there.

I follow the tall, lean, unclothed figure
hoping to be led to the garden. Room after room
we enter, never am I taken to the garden.

Some rooms have shuttered windows
where a pale light enters, walls are papered in gray.
Dust strewn floors allow our footprints to pursue us.
Her path appears marked, not to lead to the garden.
Everyone knows it exists. I catch a glimpse of yesterday
through broken shutters; she does not linger for the past.

I grow anxious, consider questions.
Perhaps she doesn't know the way
or even realize the garden is near; she may know,
preferring to go there alone. Does she
even know I'm here? She could be searching
for something that cannot be found in the garden.

I decide to ask. Perhaps I could be that something.
My mouth opens, but no words come out.
She continues leading me through empty rooms,
rooms without mirrors, without pictures, without a future . . . .

I Do Not Sleep With Strangers

Without Wings

For years they examined
the solidness of space
and determined
its source was the origin
of all things.

For the same number of years,
a dream stood at attention,
poised,
a trap ready
to unleash its power
over the aging ramparts.
A wall of pride and stoicism
built by fear
enwreathes the inhabitants
who practice with a two-way mirror
illusory perception,
a serpentine chastity belt
with a pass key—ripened fruit
glazed with desire,
a suggestion of almonds and dates
bathed in a waterfall of ancient texts.
All this
for the new order, the new
awakening.

That was their intention,
the intended target.

But
nothing was learned
from Narcissus,
and little was appropriated
from the gas ovens.

The stars will invite us back

for another tutorial session.

The lesson wasn't grasped
the first trip. And,
if not this time,
perhaps . . . our children,

if they fly. . . .

Without Feathers

All Right

Starting at the beginning is unnecessary.
Besides, it leaves more to the imagination not to.
He clings to the tri-tiered emulsion,
a cluster of gaunt-looking skulls make faces
from the towpath, jaws agape—
baby birds anticipating feeding.
Last night in a sculptured dream of a dream,
he booked a passage: the feather coming out,
slowly, ballet-like,
spreading white crystals across dark hills
whose serpentine look reveals no secret
unless the beholder is sincere.

All night, he traverses a transparent scrim
and, aboard a train of mimed gestures,
he inquires about the looseness of sunshine.
From his compartment, he sees rocks
smoothed by water masks and revelers.
Many wear the look of someone's mother,
kind and protective. Questions are answered
before they are posed, forgotten before they're asked.
He meanders about in a state of dazed refinement,
searching for a reflection or recognizable nameplate,
half expecting to hear her name or someone else's
or to pick up her scent from a discarded blouse,
a product of his unbuttoning.

Could it be this is a continuation
of something more than false starts?
Or is the clarity of consciousness
to his own weaknesses taking the place of conscience,
allowing him to live with a fair degree of comfort
without going into exile?
It's quiet now except for the wind
which issues an eerie prehistoric sound
in the pre-dawn light.

The short straw wins or is last,
depending on the point of view.
But someone must do it.
She's recruited for the mission,
the preserving.
She begins, tentatively,
securing him from moisture,
skin cracking cold, vector space
and other imponderable thoughts.
For stealing the mission,
he buttresses the elements in fifty years,
remaining in as good a shape as the night
she first assessed his memory.
Would they remain steady, clear, and circular,
smelling of secrets purchased from Woolworths?
She had to know.

A Game of Rules

Anniversary

My outstretched leg
leaves the warmth of the covers

and braves the morning cold,
but you are not here.

The smell of coffee
and bacon enters the room.

I'll pretend I'm still asleep.
How nice, you remembered

our special day.
Breakfast in bed will be fun.

Bouquet

The only effort worth making is the one it takes to learn the geography of one's own nature.

—Paul Bowles

Procesión de los Locos, San Miguel de Allende, 1991

With Mary T

Whenever I pick Mary
up in the evening,
I find her parents reading,
each sitting in a large, comfortable-
looking leather chair,
a polished mahogany table
with a large lamp between them.

And then Mary emerges
into the literary field,
her hair up
as if dressed for a showcase
occasion.

But we never discuss
books
or the lives of dead men.
Our words choose not to evaluate
the past
or construct edifices
for the future.

She's a delightful fresh-air-kind-of-girl.
We are about living,
sharing
a passage, but unaware
of the crossing.
We are like an Andrew Wyeth
still life,
enraptured with becoming itself.

1033 Kuhlman Lane
St. Louis
Summer 1962

For Deposit Only

Daybreak

The morning light
peels away the darkness—

our eyes refuel each other.
Yesterday, you were unhappy,

thinking I no longer cared for you.
You were foolish to worry.

We will share many fine moments.
Today is one of them.

Bouquet

Blessing

How the happy eyes dance!
And there's no more to eat.
Enter soon.
Somewhere, drunken pilgrims erect a ladder
from yellow fields and early planted gardens.

Sometimes, flowers bloom in the face of doubt.

The hour has long passed.
Arrange the room and prepare
the blue throne.
Absent paper whites the crown.
The head bows. Babies cry
and mothers nurse.

We must leave.

The metal stem will send us
towards cleaned hope,
amidst fluttering wings.
And it may be the summer's storm
unlocks the holy tree,
whose tower will signal the fading heart,
and the distant mountain to sing,
while the others
listen by the river,
counting orange clouds,
and the smooth, throbbing veins
of the grey stones that smile.

Jaguar Porfolio

Forgery

My feet are numb,
my eyes useless boxes.
I use my hands to walk in twilight.

A rope leads me past
the barren tree
that divides the water;
leaning towards the golden light,
its branches turn away,
forming shadows I've never seen.

Leaves surround the trunk, camouflaging
marble tablets my grandmother longed for
    me to read.
Through a throaty heat, rain walks
determined since first steps—
a passage older than writing on stone.

As night slowly opens its maximal eyes,
I feel the severe, demanding words
cutting into my fingers, instructing me—
that with his blood he had signed my name.

I Do Not Sleep With Strangers

Gypsy Girl

(Across from the Plaza of La Caridad Church
San Cristóbal de las Casas)

She wears a rose-colored dress
covered by a lime green apron.

She leans against the brown and white
sun-bleached wall of Tres Estrellas restaurant,
eating an ear of grilled corn sprinkled with paprika
and chili powder.

Her bare feet are hard, dry, and cracked.

She uses a turquoise rebozo wrapped around
her head for a turban.
Multiple eye-of-the-tiger spheres dangle
from her earlobes.

She looks as though she's from one of the caves
of the Sierra Nevada foothills near Granada,
but this ten year old Indian lives in Zinacatán,
a village in the Chiapan highlands, and speaks
Tzotzil with Spanish as a second language.

Near the curb, a few feet away, her mother and four
sisters sit in the back of a canvas-covered truck
eating their elote on a stick.

When she finishes the treat,
this gypsy will return with her mother and sisters
to her village and make more pulseras to sell
in San Cristóbal without ever thinking of Spain.

Cartouche

Outside, Wings of Mercury

At Lockwood Elementary,
after lunch
and at recess,
the game was
Pom-Pom-Pull-Away

and I was the fastest
kid in school.

At least
I liked to think so.

Alan Lamb was fast
too,
but he
never lasted as long
as I did.

Who ever started
the game would say,
"Pom-pom-pull-away"
and mention someone's name

or a group of names
and try to touch them
as they ran past.

If you were touched,
you'd join
those in the middle
and when
the spokesman called
names again

you'd try to tag
as many runners as possible

before they reached
the safety
of the other side.

Early
in the game,
the leader would call
everybody
to increase
his chances of catching
someone.

I loved it
when ten or fifteen
of them
in the middle
called my name

and I'd race
to the other end,
fainting left
then right,
side-stepping
my anxious and bewildered
peers.

Back in Mrs. McCracken's
class,
the first time
she called my name
she had me,

all
by
herself.

Cartouche

To Draw Up a Balance Sheet

And that was that.

She continued to taste the sunshine
long after he removed his lips.

Desire prolonged the hunger
as her dreams funneled her thirst
through a cave of urban alleys
littered with loaded shopping carts
on extended loan from Kmart.

Aside from nature shedding
and putting on different wraps,
the landscape remains the same:
flat, manipulated, brutalized,
desolate, and recycled.

We have such a wonderful system.
A progressive affliction.
A permanent medium at the end
of our lives, which provides little
solace or repose of mind.

We accept and turn ourselves over
like an omelette and are consumed,
each item à la carte,
except for the luncheon special.

The Old Beggar Woman

Dressed in a long, dirty dress,
a peculiar lavender hat
(shaped like Napoleon's)
which looked to be made of felt—

she approached prospective donors
and would nudge them,
and hold out her hand. Her face
assumed a pathetic expression.
Her entire appearance was woeful.

She came out of nowhere.
All of a sudden, I felt something
poking me in the side.
I turned and there was a cracked
canvas, waiting for sympathy.
I gave her 300 lira, all the change I had.
Not satisfied with my patronage
(it was early in the day),
she approached two smartly dressed Italians
who promptly told her to go to hell.

Romolo, 7 Via Porta Settimiana
Rome
10 July 1965

For Deposit Only

Translation

It's unfair when your traveling
companion gets upset with you
for saying you prefer to sleep alone.

Really.
Some things should be respected.

I'm not talking about pleasure;
I'm talking about not being taken
for granted.
All male-female relationships
are not conjugal,
even if they always seem to be.
Face it,
that's the conclusion
most people reach,
but who cares what they think?
What do they know?
Particularly when they don't know you
or even care to know me
or anything about our circumstances.

She split about an hour ago,
saying she'd see me when she saw me
or words to that effect.
It was all in sixteenth century French,
but several words hit home.

St. George Hotel
46 Norfolk Square
London
20 August 1965

For Deposit Only

With the Grain

In the shadows the room moves. Or could it be
the bedsprings? Composed within sleep's coiled tunnels,
private chambers, my spirit rises beyond the dark mountains.

No longer am I surrounded by walls I cannot embrace.
Too many fists sculpt the air, too many words cut
the silence, leaving it dripping red, a litany sung

by those who cup their ears, who ignore the screams
of dirty hands. This chorus: glimmers of glass that severs
figures of speech that entice, a web of transparent words

sung by missionaries, a scale without numbers. Confusion.
In the midst of this refuse, slow moving creatures, bewildered
by the music and searching for a place to rest, throw off

their clothing. Heat measures their steps; in hours their furrows
will be streets. A few discarded placards are read, for no good,
only more holes are formed. I avoid them by climbing into a loft

where belief, unlike language isn't questioned. I see empty shelves,
pallid and stretched, losing shape. Do I look strange?
I approach mirrors, but they turn away, entranced with incestuous

passion, inbred reflections. Below, behind a marble statue,
a fire casts ripples of orange, fingers scratch away
at the darkness, reducing distances. Naked figures

meander among the broken columns, scour the ground,
wanting to replace. There are no sides left to take in these unfilled
spaces. It is a question of light whose moment will come.

When it falls, I will have forgotten all of them.

I Do Not Sleep With Strangers

Timepiece

The clock's pulse
is strong, unfaltering
and unexcitable—
even without hands

all moments
are treated impartially,
unemotionally,
and pass unnoticed. . . .

Blind,
not masked like Justice
or discouraged;
appeals are not acknowledged—

all decisions . . . final.

131 Selden
Galesbury, Il
23 March 1972

For Deposit Only

Skin Deep

Bananas
are fun
to
un
dress

Peeling
off
your things
is
better

I
like
natural
fruit
flavor

Bouquet

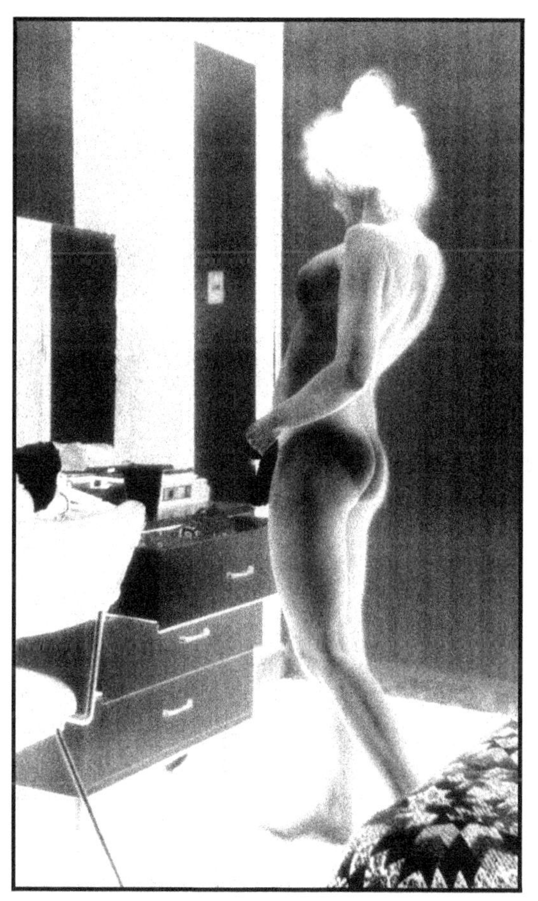

Together

They enter the shop
Sitting at a
rear table
they order lunch
She is well-dressed
he is well-dressed
His eyes look tired
her eyes look tired
He talks of her children
she talks of his children
It's a good lunch
says she
Yes a fine lunch
says he
He talks of his children
she talks of her children
they talk of their children
Would you like dessert
he asks
Yes please
This is good
she says
Excellent
says he
She once made him feel
like Adonis
her hands moving
shaping his body
He blooms
each year for her
the hooded-red anemone
the windflower
Together they leave
the shop

Criterion

A closed door confronts me

and then it slowly,
gradually opens.
Why does this movement occur?
To encourage me to step forward

and look inside?
Is this an act of introduction,
an invitation to a beginning,

a singular opportunity for our exchange?
What can be found in this well-lit room?
The same that I encountered in the others?

Or will it be something unusual—
a chorus of orchids blooming,
or something spontaneous,

a roman candle
pin-pointing the Big Dipper?
I have seen those

who refer to themselves as *Mystery* . . .
and I have aligned scores of the little pieces,
but my question lingers.

Does every meeting denote a puzzle
to be analyzed and taken apart
before the sections can embrace,

producing a phase called love?

Bouquet

Panajachel, Guatemala

The launch takes an hour to cross
the lake to San Pedro
and about the same to reach Santiago Atitlán.
Early in the day, the crossing glides.
Coming back,
the water reached up for us
as we tried to embrace the low flying clouds.

When I look at her picture,
her eyes looking back into mine,
I wonder
how long can I remain objective.
No shard of evidence exists
to confirm my prognosis.
But for how long?
The few rough lines in the notebook
represent a full conceptual cycle.
There will be more than traces
of aesthetic exploration.
I must experience the object,
not artify it.

The sun bites down hard on the flowers
and continues bleaching the animal skulls
hanging on the brick wall of the patio garden.

The tomato plants no longer produce.

Every time I return to the States,
life unfolds so cleanly.
I am going to put the third world on hold.
I can go back without going back,
travel wherever I want.
I'll sit in my patio and imagine at my own speed.

Cartouche

Letters

I hear your heart crying
as it loses its grip, withering to a gravel bed. Here I walk
without fear of being followed, examining stones,
smooth as your face, quiet as the calm
which separates us from the opaque spaces of a storm
that carried our excitement through dense jungles—
          an exotic season.

The air is still.
Waves of heat serpentine to a cloudless blue.
I hear a field mouse gasp as a hawk grabs its back, interrupting
its silent prayer, its shrinking shadow a final offering.

Two scorpions emerge
from the cracked lips and perform a pas de deux under the sun's
harsh spotlight. Their steps choreograph words you wrote to me
from the green isles. I fear these tales as much as I did yours
and seek the other side of the river bed where,
under a singular cloud's umbrella, I reflect upon all you've said.

I'm no longer in stillness.
The wind chases dust, the bright light serves as a page
for my reverie. This music creates thirst for a lullaby
and I drift along the wall's coolness. A raven tells me
transparency is a lure and offers the secret of the wishing well
if I promise to tell no one where we've been.

I Do Not Sleep With Strangers

Departure

She left the room
without looking back,
without saying goodbye.

Why do people leave pretending
they are not hurting, too?
It's time to meet someone else.

She left the door wide open . . .
someone could walk in.
Maybe I'll go out, look around,

check the scene, so to speak.

Bouquet

Room in White Sheets

My brain, invaded by your lines,
refuses to perform its functions . . . .
I invite the vast night to yield
to my beckoning. . . .

Tired of shadows,
my mood closes its arms and walks
into the cave . . . where—

Do you ever consider breaking
your affliction like Greek dancers
who smash wine glasses

to escape being alone?

I have envisioned my words,
traveling as a sun
where moments are irresistibly spun,
where one separates
ornament from trinket of logic,
rejecting the metronome's timed meaning.

Do I still have it in me
to dive into a pile of leaves?

A Game of Rules

Anti-History

Red stones lie
unvexed
in a dry river
bed.
They were bone
white.
Each day,
each night,
red stones
and
bleached bones
bed together
without
regard to gender.
Low hanging
clouds
meander,
bandages of self-
inflicted wounds,
as I skim this
modern translation.

Without Feathers

Involuntary

The fingers of the tree
wear no rings
in mourning the loss

of your dream.

Its palm expresses
the seasons, its feet,
miles of unrecorded experience.

And with iris wide
open,
its eyes continue
to blink, registering
each lie,

while the river supports
new payload
and meanders to the sea
without bitterness,
without remorse,
remembering

the garden was good once.

Without Feathers

Candy

When I opened the door to my efficiency,
her right hand was behind her back.
"Here, this is for you," she said,
extending a Mercedes Benz hood ornament
suspended on a red ribbon.

I first saw her in the Cine Art
ticket booth in Gaslight Square.
I'd come to see Godard's *Breathless*
(*A Bout de Souffle*). When she handed me
my ticket, she said, "You'll like this,
it's your kind of film."
I took a close look at this girl
under a black beret, brown page-boy
hair. She was right. I liked
Truffaut's story and Belmondo & Seberg.

The next time I saw her, she was sitting
on the lawn outside of Brookings Hall.
I was on my way to Smith's Art
History class. As I passed, she said,
"Would you like some chocolate?"
I accepted her offer. She said
she'd like to see where I lived.
I gave her my address, told her
to drop by, evenings were best.

Tonight she wore black slacks
and a man's white button-down.
The whites of her eyes were clear—
peace flags—
her pupils, two huge caverns
encouraging exploration.
I hung my new Mercedes on the coat hook
behind the door. On the radio,
Frank crooned *Strangers in the Night*.

She sat on the side of the bed
and picked up one of my poems
I had fantailed on the white bedspread.
"Are these precious?" she asked.
"No," I responded. "Not at all."
I poured her a glass of Moulin-à-Vent.

She swallowed the wine and licked
her lips, slowly.
She had a poem about sharing
in her left hand.
She reached to the right and turned
off the radio,
the lamp on the headboard.
The street light on Clara
became a candle in my room.
She smiled, wet her lips,
stood,
and removed her shirt,
her slacks,
white panties.
And from her purse, extracted
a tiny silver box.
She opened the box and placed a small,
white pill
on the tip of her pink tongue.

710 Clara
St. Louis
17 October 1966

For Deposit Only

Not Everyone Dances

What is freedom
unless one can express all sentiments?

Do we fool ourselves when we assume
different roles and act out parts to show
our tolerance and understanding of other cultures?

As we dance, a few people watch us.
Others talk among themselves.

Many don't even know we are dancing
and they stand nearby and cannot hear
thc different voices in our song.

Is that simply destiny?

No matter who beats the drum only a few
listeners actually hear it and even fewer

interpret the message of the touched skin.

Fetus

Without walls,
the room will prosper.
Bleached white and picked clean
by vultures,
the skeleton performs
a nimble dance
to a chorus of acid rain.

Do not tease me
with your smiles and gestures.
I want to trust.
Peel back deceit.
Trash it.

Incinerate.

Waves lull me
beyond relaxation;
eager clouds soften the way,
sharing dreams,
molding desire.

Each movement vibrates the web.
Surprise is not a tactic.

I want to build
a beginning.

Let's use our hands,
winnow the choices.

We must not waiver

once we decide to open.

Cartouche

Blackbird

Since prehistoric times
these creatures have flown
with few restrictions,
observing . . . .

They have seen it all
and within each country
our struggle remains.

Always there are those
who want to limit
others,

to define what is best,
to determine the path
others must walk.

We don't learn.

Diérèse

Emotion

A breath of smoke,
my face revealed.

A mask of motion,
my wind, my life

dispersed,

here, there,
nowhere, everywhere.

A mask, my face,
a breath, my life,
the wind—

all directions.

New England Tennis Camp
Cheshire, CT
9 July 1968

For Deposit Only

The Passing of Light

There is no signature

on the bottom line,
only the date
    marking the passing.

A boy dies,
a girl dies,

old men, women,
all races—
an assortment of colors.

Death is a rainbow—

the white light gone.

4341 Grand Ave.
Des Moines
17 June 1974

For Deposit Only

T'ho

(The very noble and loyal city of Mérida)

The mucky weather hangs on my skin
but doesn't pull me down.

Houston has acclimated me.

The taxi is a VW van with TV
and a swinging Cristo on a chain.
The driver moves his massive round head
slowly, side to side,
scanning the late evening traffic;
could just be a trance.
His Mayan beak analyzes
the air as if expecting something new,
a different ingredient or a hint
that rain marches to the Yucatán.
His long teeth are stained,
his guayabera pale blue.

At the Posada Toledo we examine three rooms,
none clean, one a.c. works well.
We replace a fluorescent light which reveals
more dirt. Good shower.

Sat. 9:40 hotel breakfast room. I order
hot cakes. No batter.
Have French toast instead.
I find the coffee disappointingly weak.
We consider changing hotels.
Fernando, the concierge, wants to show us
a suite, but it's occupied another day.

Time to explore.

A body blur speeds past at 61 Esperanza
as Yucatecans press for the blue and white
#8 bus. A pink dressed señora pushes her way on.

A two-year-old lunches on mother's right breast.
No perspiration streams from any of these bodies.

Heading toward the market
the day's heart pumps a blazing chalky light.

Cartouche

Good Day

The day beckons.
The rain has stopped—

Fresh air, a crispness,
enriches my lungs,

lubricating deep to my soul.
I accept the invitation

and mount
the first gliding feather—

hands free of reins,
hot coals kindle my thirst.

710 Clara
St. Louis
5 September 1966

For Deposit Only

Siempre Nuevo

Un amor sincero
no muere
ni se puede apagar
    u olvidarse

Existe siempre
reside en el corazón
está encerrado en el alma
    que lo recuerda
como algo especial

y tal vez
tal vez
renace

Panajachel, Guatemala
4 July 1990

Jaguar Porfolio

Therapy

Incense fills the room—

affection encourages affection.

Soft words introduce foreplay—

postponed . . .

while others sit drinking,
listening to Ravi's fiery sitar,
laughing with the water pipe,

dazed by the smoke and bubbles

controlling their wide, red eyes.

710 Clara
St. Louis
23 September 1966

For Deposit Only

Curves to Amber

I can't read the words
behind the smoked glass.
I know of no pain against the skin
like geothermal maga spewing and exploding
its molten fluids, penetrating my pores, destroying the viscera,
leaving angst and despair in neon numbers. Who knew?

A tiny seed erupts
causing aches deeper than doubt.
A new struggle pushes forth,
living without love, no ground-breaking ceremonies—
the pain of living without sharing or being in communion.

Still, I knew you'd phone me.
I know of no other touch so close
to the edge of letting go.
From the embryo through the reflection,
each wave of water crashes against our sorrow and pain.

Poised, you turn away without emotion,
a glittering orange gem, unobtainable,
impressive as an emperor brimming with heart.

I'm bleeding from my eyes.
I have no clear path through this craziness.
The road swells into a sponge highway.

Night rhythms clear a space to dance.
We sway in the summer breeze, emotion crammed
in a beer can, never arriving on the other side.

Soon, dust gathers like a fragrant tiger lily
sinking deeply, past the glare, littering my niche,
never letting go, confirming reality

among the hosts, pronouncing the final good-bye.

Lighthouse

The touching
of our skin

on skin,
a kiss,

an embrace,
clarifies

embedded acts—
a phosphorescent

image,
your forest,

a thick tattoo,
a neon-lit cave—

a beacon
to safe harbor.

Pull me in.

710 Clara
St. Louis
6 October 1966

For Deposit Only

Empty Morning

Today, I flavor
my coffee with tears.

You were unfair
to leave me

without a warning,
without a kiss.

Finding you gone
and cold sheets

as a memento
made getting up

even harder.
It's so unlike you

to leave me alone
to embrace the new day.

Bouquet

A Cluster of Truth Shadows

A path coils like it recognizes
the yellow-green cavern from photographs
of our galaxy, stamped
to the uneven gouging of a black rose.

Leaves whisper the passing.

A dark line lingers behind us;
we turn around and walk it.

It feels like someone is stirring
us with a long, wooden ladle. No one

sees me, head bowed in a stream,
watching the rocks release ancient reserves
of moonlight, overheating the visible spectrum of trees.

I sprinkle pollen on pouty lips and lick them.

Yellow tumors zigzag
                                        when you open
your hood of erogenous laments. Where I once

saw only straw . . .
              a smell of mushrooms
                                        with self-conscious ignorance
swaddling its own universe; the web glistens—
language stumbles . . . .

I see the trunks where you store all that you are
away into the least thing you do
                                        for safe keeping,
for someone special, no doubt. Others

watch the trail and sniff limbs
without touching. Feathered and furry creatures chatter.

To reach you requires an understanding of prehistoric
semantics pulled from behind bougainvillea.

Forgetting the moment,
for a moment, the sun in your eyes forces us to dim our
strobes to balance your burden, lost as you are
in helplessly complex assembled shadings.

I do not believe your zone can rise
with semen on your hands and clothes.
It's a little too clammy and others will notice.

You're still there, of course, anxious
to spill yourself over a mountain of bones and forests,
leaving us, tattooed by passion,
humming an empty, glowing canvas.

Live Ivory

I showed her my carved ivory ball—
spheres within spheres.
Intricate moments of entrances
    and exits.
I let her hold it,
look inside, and feel its Chinese edges.
She couldn't see the smoke
or hear the elephant's trumpet.
But, after all,
she doesn't know me very well.

A Weekend in Montauk

I looked at my watch—
already 8 a.m.

I'd slept late,
but I had no reason
to get up;
I was on a break.

I'd stayed up past one
talking to
Marsha,
listening to her
Johnny Mathis collection
which
she'd inherited
from her mom.

I got up,
showered
and dressed,
decided to see
what was going on.

Walked down the hall
past her parent's
bedroom,
the door was half-open,
looked in,
Mrs. Spicer was in a bra,
stepping into white
panties.

She looked up.

Sorry,
I said.

She smiled,
said,
It's okay.

I continued to
Marsha's room,
heard the Spoonful
singing *Summer in the City*,
came to her open
door,
looked in.

She was nude,
sitting on her bed
combing her wet hair.
Excuse me,
I said.
Marsha smiled,
raised her shoulders
along with
her small breasts
and said,
That's okay.

I walked into the
kitchen,
poured a cup of
coffee,

pleased
everything was going okay.

Cartouche

One Way to Say Good-bye

It was seven-thirty on a Sunday morning
in June, my father's second life
beginning, my mother's too,
though she didn't want to admit it.
My sister and her husband, still in bed,
heard Mom pleading in the family room.

"Can't we talk about this? Please . . .
whatever it is, we can work it out.
You can't just leave. I beg you."

"There's nothing to work out.
I'm sorry. I've made up my mind.
I'm going."

"Talk to me at least. Please.
Don't go. We can do something.
Tell me, what it is, what's wrong?
Don't throw thirty-one years away.
If it's something with me . . . talk
about it, tell me, I'm willing
to change. Anything."

"You'll need to go in and sign
the papers. There's nothing more
to say or discuss.
I don't love you. I'm leaving."

The night before, they'd fixed popcorn
and looked at family slides:
Mom on the swivel bar stool
next to Dad,
Lei Lane and Gene on the hardwood floor,
looking up at the portable memory
screen—
laughing at the changes,

mostly, each at his own,
discussing, recalling the trips,
like the one to the petrified forest,
which was a major disappointment,
seeing rocks two to four inches high,
hardly a tall forest frozen in time.

Many events were almost forgotten—
fading as the blue Ektachromes
flashing before them.
No one had noticed or thought
anything of the neat little stacks
Dad was making, separating the pictures,
placing some in a different box
from the others.

The morning sun burned strong
and hot when he drove away,
like the fire he'd left
sizzling inside 501 Hillside Drive.
The brown Plymouth Scamp pulled
a small U-Haul,
packed with a few clothes . . .
the racket stringing machine,
and a small box of Ektachromes.

American Poetry Confronts the 1990s

GREENPEACE
BICENTENNIAL
enfant terrible
Harry Burrus
Fountain View
TX 77057
SAN MIGUEL ALLENDE
GTO., MEXICO 37700
PRINTED
BELGIQUE

Author Introductions

For Deposit Only: Selected Poems 1960–1975

Each of the time frames in this collection conjures up special and not so special memories. I'm 15 when the first section begins and 31 in the last. A considerable physical and mental leap. Well, physical at least.

During this fifteen year stretch, I lived in St. Louis; San Antonio; Europe; Cheshire, CT; Fairfield, Iowa; Iowa City; Galesburg, IL; and Des Moines. From my wardrobe, I chose the costumes of student teacher, teacher; filmmaker, traveler, and tennis pro. The tennis shorts generated the most activity. Jeans and khakis when I traveled.

Early on, particularly with tennis tournaments and travel, I recorded my observations. I developed the habit of logging names of restaurants, menu items, vintages of wine, names of bars, hotels, cities, and streets. As a teenager, tennis saturated my summers. At out of town tournaments, I frequently received housing. That's when members of the tournament committee or members of the host club or organization put a player up in their home. Usually, the member had a son or daughter entered in the tournament, although not always. Sometimes, my host was just a tennis patron. I made a point of investigating wine cellars and liquor cabinets. I'd leaf through photo albums to see where they'd been. I'd write down their style of china and crystal, the brand of silverware, not anticipating I'd use this information later as a tennis pro to utilize the time picking up balls during and between, and after a lesson.

I mention all of this, not because it's forthcoming in the poems, but to explain how my writing began. And, I should say, at no point, even during my French period when I had a French friend and read French and other European poets and writers, did I think of my work appearing in book form. From this stretch, only once, in the mid-sixties, did I bother to submit material, and that was to the *Yale Series of Younger Poets*. My manuscript poems were on different colors of paper, each color chosen to reinforce the mood and attitude of the poem. James Tate won that year.

So, for my friends, readers, critics, historians, and the rest, here is *For Deposit Only*, a chit of those early, formative (?) years.

1 June 1990

Jaguar Porfolio: poems retrieved

Friends frequently ask me about the early work, poems written in the sixties and early seventies. But since it is only in the last five years that my poems have been published in books, these publications largely reflect immediate adventures. Although I am not so sure there has been much, if any, thematic change from the earlier period, certainly some recent poems are more abstract and less linear than their antecedents.

For Deposit Only: Selected Poems 1960-1975 addressed the issue of early writing and represented much of what I had held on to for over thirty years, going back to some poems written in high school. Recently, however, my poetry chest was augmented.

In the early seventies, I played a tennis tournament in San Luis Potosí, Mexico, during Semana Santa (Holy Week). The competition was stiff; yearly the tournament attracted an international crowd. Part of the allure for me was as long as I remained in the tournament, my hotel room was paid for by the tournament's foreign players committee which existed to promote the annual event and to attract players from other countries. Furthermore, every evening, at the Club de Deportivo, the tournament offered some kind of entertainment or dinner for the players and their friends.

I somehow managed to stay alive in the tournament for the first three or four days, sometimes longer. And with much of the room bill covered, the other days were easily worth the added expense because I viewed this period as a much needed change from the cold, snow, and wind-chill factors of Iowa and Illinois.

I've noticed, for the most part, when traveling I write about things I am not immediately experiencing; the exotic environment stimulates the writing process and helps distill my objectivity and, further, acts as a memory filter, clearing the glass on events a year or two old or older. Little of the writing I did during these tournaments is about Mexico or tennis. That would come later.

I'd write a few lines before or during breakfast, sometimes at the club waiting for my next match, but usually sitting in one of the city's plazas. When I stayed at the Hotel Principal I'd start at the Plazuela del Carmen then walk to the Plaza San Francisco or Plaza de los Panadores. Mostly, I made my journal entries in tiny restaurants like the Noche y Día—where three of us got sick from chicken noodle soup—and in bars.

And it was at the Jaguar one night a group of us elected to hit one more bar before getting something to eat at La Virreina, along with La Lonja, a favorite restaurant of mine. After dinner we'd visit other cantinas. I had a notebook of poems with me I was shaping into a collection tentatively called *Masks*. I didn't want to keep up with the black binder, so, I left it with one of the bartenders.

I forgot about leaving it at the Jaguar that night. I had other poems in my room I was working on and the notebook never crossed my mind until many years later. I just assumed the poems were lost. Several months back I decided to give it a shot and wrote the club, the foreign players' coordinator, and the bar, hoping to garner several sleuths into looking for the notebook, thinking all the time there was no way it was still there. Fortunately, I was wrong. I received the binder seven and a half weeks later. Much of what follows is from the *Jaguar Porfolio*. Perhaps it's time to play San Luis Potosí again.

24 March 1991

Notes

Many poems in this collection are from the following publications:

A Game of Rules. Black Tie Press, Houston, 1989.
American Poetry Confronts the 1990s. Black Tie Press, Houston, 1990, 1991.
Blackbird 10. Blackbird Institute, Baltimore, 2012.
Bouquet. Black Tie Press, Houston, 1989.
Cartouche. Black Tie Press, Houston, 1995.
Diérèse #47 Winter. Paris, France, 2009.
For Deposit Only: Selected Poems 1960-1975. Black Tie Press, Houston, 1990.
Friour Review #10. Brussels, Belgium, 2009.
I Do Not Sleep With Strangers: Confessions of a Tennis Pro. Black Tie Press, Houston, 1987.
Jaguar Porfolio: Poems Retrieved. Black Tie Press, Houston, 1991.
Offerta Speciale. Turin, Italy, 1990s.
Without Feathers. Black Tie Press, Houston, 1990.

Main title page glyph: Nagual.
Glyphs in order of appearance: Night; Vulture; Grasp; Star; Water; Jaguar; Flint Blade; Year; and Ruler.

Rock Art: Warrior Poet.

TIME PASSES LIKE RAIN

a novel
(synopsis)

Harry Burrus

Laura Ryder, an expat English poet, journeys with two adventurous female friends to a small South American country, their sights set on trekking through the rain forest and climbing the country's highest mountain, ostensibly to see how well they respond to the challenges nature throws at them.

They arrive in the capital city amidst protests and violent demonstrations over the recent Presidential Election. Through their interactions with a wealthy inland landowner, a newspaper editor, and a famous actress, they eventually become entangled in a web of political turmoil, exposing themselves to murder, kidnapping, and physical atrocities.

Nevertheless, they extricate themselves, determined to pursue their original goal. Hiring porters and a guide, they embark on their trek through one of South America's largest rain forests and find themselves on a roller coaster of experiences ranging from the enlightening to the horrifying. They befriend and hunt with Amerindians and fight for their lives against hostile indigenous tribes and illegal gold miners. At the same time, they are faced with combating the natural obstacles of extreme heat, rain, humidity, black caimans, and pit vipers, making them question the wisdom of their journey and whether they will survive.

http://www.amazon.com/Time-Passes-Like-Rain-novel/dp/1890279935/ref=sr_1_1?s=books&ie=UTF8&qid=1336144400&sr=1-19

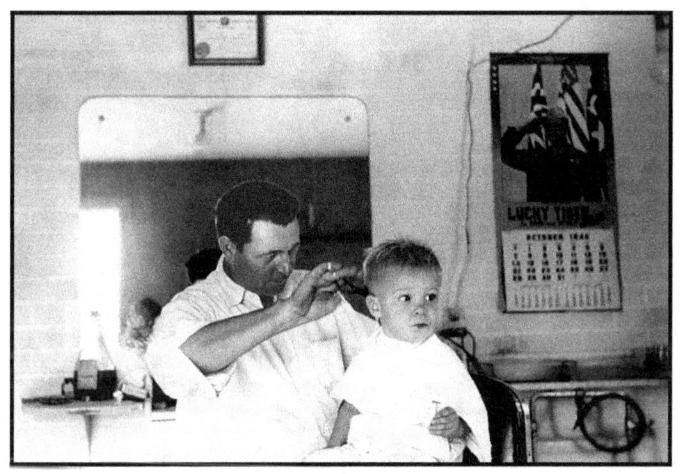

First Professional Haircut, San Antonio, Texas

Harry Burrus grew up in St. Louis, Missouri. Harry has advanced degrees in Writing, Film and Communication Studies and is an avid traveler.

As a tennis pro in Des Moines, Iowa, he hosted his own television show, "Tennis Tips With Harry Burrus." He played international tennis and, at one time, World Tennis Magazine ranked Harry and his father number two in the United States in Father & Son Doubles.

Harry had a one-man exhibition at Houston's International FotoFest in which dozens of his photographs were displayed. His photographs and collages have appeared in exhibitions in Russia, Europe, and South America. He has written a novel (*Time Passes Like Rain*), eight collections of poetry, eight plays, numerous screenplays, and several articles about the Beats (Kerouac, Burroughs, Ginsberg, and Cassady) in Mexico which appeared in *Beatdom* and the UK publication *Beat Scene*. Harry is the writer-director of the feature film *Marrakech*:

Examples of his work can be seen at
http://sites.google.com/site/hburrus/

Alyscamps Press: Paris

Available & Forthcoming Titles for 2013

Charles Bukowski, Henry Miller & the Bluebird of Love by Karl Orend.

Elegy on the Closing of the French Brothels by Lawrence Durrell.

Henry Miller's Angelic Clown by Karl Orend.

Je t'aime...moi non plus: Introducing Monsieur Serge Gainsbourg by Karl Orend.

Paris Revisited (New Special Edition) by Anaïs Nin. Extensive Afterword by leading historian of expatriate Paris, Karl Orend.

&

Collected Essays on Louis-Ferdinand Céline by Pascal Pia.

Jérôme Lindon by Jean Echenoz.

Louis-Ferdinand Céline in a Brown Shirt by H. E. Kaminsk.

Models of Madness: Four Nightmare Visions of America by Gershon Legman.

The Genesis of Tropic of Cancer by Michael Fraenkel.

The Paris Poems of Ted Joans.

Tropic of Cancer by Mario Vargas Llosa.

For Alyscamps titles, including out of print titles,
contact Alyscamps at Alyscampspressparis@gmail.com

www.ingramcontent.com/pod-product-compliance
Lightning Source LLC
LaVergne TN
LVHW050625100826
845148LV00011B/1730

* 9 7 8 0 6 1 5 6 3 0 4 5 8 *